Cali

Jarrold Publishing

CONTENTS

Introduction to California   3
A colourful history   7
First and foremost: recreation   11
Bears, whales, hummingbirds and sequoias   13
Before you take the wheel – a note
   for visitors from overseas   15
Visitors' guide to food and drink in California   16
Don't forget your fig-leaf!   20
Where to stay   20

Hints for your holiday   22
Where to go and what to see   23
San Francisco   23
The green north of California   47
Through the Sierra Nevada   54
Death Valley and other deserts   63
San Diego   70
Los Angeles   74
America's dream road   85
The Central Valley   89

Useful things to know   90
Index   95

Maps and plans
San Francisco   24
San Francisco Bay   43
Northern California   49
Sierra Nevada   55
Southern California   62
Death Valley   65
Los Angeles   76
The coast between Los Angeles and San Francisco   85
General map   back cover

Title page: Yosemite National Park

Coronado Bridge from the beach, San Diego

Introduction to California

You are on your way to the land of gold!

Each of the fifty federal states in the USA has an unofficial as well as an official name. New York, for example, calls itself the 'Empire State', neighbouring New Jersey is the 'Garden State', and Mississippi is the 'Magnolia State'. These are festive names, slogans for the many parades held in each state, for car licence plates or for special-issue stamps. Flamboyant, jocular even, they reflect a taste for good-natured self-congratulation.

California, however, calls itself simply *The Golden State*. The meaning of this unofficial title is not immediately apparent, since California is not golden in any obvious sense. Well, all right, the sunsets over the Pacific Ocean sometimes have a golden tinge. The sand dunes in the desert regions sometimes shimmer in a dull golden haze. The oranges and peaches that grow in the Central Valley have a reddish-gold hue. Is that it? No. The word 'golden' is to be taken literally, as a perpetual reminder of the roar with which the remote, sparsely populated, mountainous state on the far western coast of the North American continent suddenly erupted into history.

'Gold found in California' screamed the headlines in New York, Chicago and New Orleans. Men who had nothing particular to do, or who did not know exactly how to make their first million, or else were being hotly pursued by the sheriff, packed their bags, bought themselves spades, sieves and pans and hurried west, over prairies, salt deserts and the Rocky Mountains to the Pacific Coast. The year was 1848.

The first wave of gold prospectors hit California in 1849. What happened next is familiar from Wild West movies: the honest men among the many villains, those who were quickest on the draw, who avoided being scalped by Indians on the way, who did not succumb to moonshine whisky and loose women, and then finally wooed the finest girl for miles around, men of this stamp stayed and became the founders of modern California.

There was gold in abundance; there was timber and fish, and the land was astonishingly fertile. The climate was dependable, pleasantly cool in the north and pleasantly warm in the south. Those who found the perilous drudgery in the gold-fields uncongenial could go into business, grow vegetables or build houses for the thousands of people who each year took the advice commonly given at that time: 'Go west, young man, go west.'

The states on the Atlantic seaboard of the USA had all begun as small, God-fearing colonies, firmly controlled by the colonial power, England. They had to fight a bloody revolution in order to gain their independence. Then came a senseless civil war. California had things easier.

There was no war. The United States had to exercise its authority over Mexico, but there was hardly any shooting in California. When the altercation was over, it was quietly agreed that the United States should take California.

Where else could you find such a thing – a paradise where there has never been a war? At a stroke, the paradise called California was both famous and prosperous; the magnificent city of San Francisco was built almost from scratch, there was gold and oil, vines and palms grew, and the whole place was bursting with energy and elation, life and youthfulness. A golden state indeed!

And California has remained pretty much the same. It is still a paradise for young people, for the wealthy, for mountaineers, surfers, hunters, nature-lovers, holiday-makers and students. And for jewellers. And air-force pilots. And Chinese cooks. And visionaries. And painters. Nowhere else in the USA are there so many Porsches darting down the freeways. Nowhere else are there so many hang-gliders. And nowhere else are people as friendly, free and easy and helpful.

California, which in 1850 became the thirty-first state of the Union, has provided several presidents and plays an important role in elections – it is the most populous state in the USA, with more than 24 million inhabitants. No other state supplies the country with such prodigal amounts of vitamins as California – in the form of oranges, green salad, almonds, olives, nuts, plums, lemons, hops, carrots and peaches, all of which reach the peak of perfection here.

Climatically, California can be divided into two parts: the southern two-thirds, where sunshine is guaranteed, and the north, where growth is guaranteed. The north is mainly green, moistened by the Pacific winds, to which the state owes not only the giant redwood trees, thousands of years old, but also the new wealth of its vineyards.

Southern California, however, shimmers in all the colours of the rainbow. On Sunset Boulevard the spindly palms flutter above the hullabaloo of Hollywood; in Yosemite the best mountaineers in America scale the sheer, smooth walls of the gigantic granite cliffs; in San Diego the dolphins distribute kisses at Sea World; in Six Flags passengers on the world's largest roller-coaster scream for their lives as they hurtle vertically downwards. And over and over again, the many radio stations play

Yosemite National Park

the unofficial state anthem, the melodic hit tune with the refrain 'It never rains in Southern California'.

Well, almost never. The seasons in California are not as punctilious as in Europe or in the Atlantic states of the USA. Nor are there really four seasons, but actually only two – a wet winter season and a long dry season that lasts for the rest of the year. In the north-west there is abundant rainfall, and in the southern deserts virtually none, except when one of the terrifying summer thunderstorms sends flood waters foaming violently through the dried-out canyons. The climate along the long coastline is mild, in the high Sierra Nevada it is harsher; in the higher deserts it is bearable, and in the lower deserts a foretaste of the fires of hell.

California is one of the richest states of the Union. About half of its total income is generated by new, high-tech industries. Silicon Valley has come to symbolise the entire computer and electronics industry. And with so much high-tech industry, military research and production are never far away. San Diego, Long Beach and San Francisco are important ports for the US navy, the infantry trains at Fort Ord, and the air force has large bases in California, notably Vandenberg Air Force Base. Vandenberg is the second most important rocket-launching base in America, after Cape Canaveral in Florida. Other contributors to California's wealth include agriculture, fishing, tourism, printing, and the chemical, timber and textile industries. And then of course there is Hollywood and the entertainment industry: this is the cinema capital of the world, where you wouldn't go to see cathedrals, but where some of the main attractions are the palaces where Humphrey Bogart, Clark Gable and Rita Hayworth once lived.

A casual glance at a map of California might give the impression that this is an uncommonly devout region, and fairly Iberian in character. The three largest cities are called Los Angeles, San Diego and San Francisco, and there follows an endless litany of saints and martyrs – Santa Barbara and Santa Monica, San Buenaventura and San Fernando, San José de Guadalupe and San Juan Capistrano, Santa Clara and Santa Cruz. California's place-names commemorate half the Catholic sainthood. The somewhat out-of-the-way state capital has the most pious name of all – Sacramento.

These names are the only surviving reminders of California's Spanish heritage, apart from the rough stone mission buildings. The former legitimate owners of California's hunting grounds – the Indians – left nothing behind.

The geography of California appears simple: the state rises in the west out of the ocean, stark and extremely dramatic in the north, gentler and sandy in the south. A range of hills, the Coast Range, runs all the way along the coast. The eastern border is also formed by mountains, the forbidding granite barrier of the Sierra Nevada. In between is the Central Valley, California's treasure-house, which runs for 400 miles (700 km) from north to south and is one of the most fertile areas of the continent.

The state borders are dead straight, as if the surveyors had grown tired of following the untamed twists and turns of tumbling streams or the zigzag of mountain ridges. The borders with the neighbouring states of Oregon and Nevada seem to have been drawn with a ruler, as does that with Mexico, the former homeland. Only the border with Arizona looks natural – it follows the course of the mighty Colorado River.

And what do Californians look like? Blond? Suntanned? Do they speak a Californian dialect? Do they cook Californian food? In short, are Californians noticeably Californian?

Well, 65% of the population is white, 8% is black, and the largest minority group is Hispanic – immigrants from Mexico and other Central American countries, who originally came as seasonal workers to wealthy California and remained to fight tenaciously for equality; strikes by market-garden workers or orange-pickers can seriously affect America's vitamin consumption. Because California is America's so-called gateway to the East, Japan, China, Korea, Vietnam and the Philippines have in the course of the past hundred years added about a million citizens to the state's population. Despite this cosmopolitan mixture, California has certain characteristics that are peculiarly its own, ranging from the broad slang through the cuisine, with its Spanish-Mexican influences, to its cheerful music. California is permanent propaganda for the 'sunny side of life'.

However, every paradise has concealed within it a highly explosive apple-tree, and under the glittering, smiling, joyous, luxurious surface of Californian life lurks the threat of disaster. In 1812 southern California was devastated by a massive earthquake, in 1868 and 1872 the earth and the mountains rumbled, and the great 'quake of 1906 almost wiped the beautiful city of San Francisco off the map. Ever since then, California has lived in the certain knowledge that another big 'quake was on its way. And indeed, on October 17th 1989, it came: a severe earthquake, recorded at 7.1 on the Richter scale, shook San Francisco, causing considerable loss of life and damage to buildings in some areas.

Nevertheless, California epitomises the American dream, a tangible vision of unlimited space, natural beauty, progress and wealth, of climbers conquering granite mountains, of sailing and surfing in the foaming Pacific breakers, of the glowing purity of the desert. The dream of freedom, of a better world.

🗿 A colourful history

The California Gold Rush

If you, as a visitor to the holiday state of California, would like to note just one name from the state's history, you would be well advised to choose John Sutter. Every child from Eureka to San Diego has heard of him – and of his glittering, adventurous, desperately sad story which changed the course of Californian history right up to the present day.

'General' Sutter, a native of Switzerland, amassed great wealth in the Mexican province of California from his vast herds of cattle, a whisky distillery, shops, a blacksmith's forge, a blanket factory, a tannery and a mill. The Mexican governor of California said to him, 'Señor Sutter, you should fortify your ranch, you never know what the Indians might be up to. Or the English. Or those Yankees. You understand?'

So John Sutter had part of his estate in the Sacramento Valley, which he called 'New Helvetia', reconstructed like a fortress. Tree trunks were rammed into the ground, a weapons store was built, an observation tower erected and the heavy gate bolted at night. The estate was rechristened Sutter's Fort.

General Sutter summoned his foreman, James Marshall. 'Listen, Marshall,' he said, 'make sure that the slope for the new mill stream is dug properly. If it's too steep, the water will sweep away the mill in the spring.' So James Marshall went away and inspected the new ditch. The date of this order is known, so profound did the consequences prove to be: it was January 24th 1848.

For when Mr Marshall came to the bed of the stream, he saw a few curious yellow specks in the gravel. They gleamed. They glinted in the sun, like gold. It *was* gold!

Marshall ran back to his boss. 'For heaven's sake', shouted the General, 'keep your mouth shut! Don't tell a soul about the gold. Not a soul!' But the secret could not be kept. Sutter's cowboys deserted their cattle and began to dig. The workers in the tannery left the hides to rot and began to dig. The whisky in the distillery turned

Sutter's Fort, Sacramento

Cabrillo Monument, San Diego

sour. Strangers rushed in and burrowed like wild animals in the new stream bed, making it completely unusable. They could all think of only one thing – gold.

In San Francisco harbour sailors ran from the ships and rushed up the Sacramento River; it is said that 500 abandoned ships were soon blocking the port. And because newspapers throughout the world were full of the inexhaustible gold seams of California, sending hundreds of thousands of adventurers from all over the place hurrying to the west coast of America and up the Sacramento River, a new name was needed for this frenzy: the California Gold Rush!

1849! Mr Sutter, on whose land the first gold had been found, was powerless against the invading gold-diggers. Tent cities shot up overnight. The Colts smoked. Prices rocketed. Washington's designs on the Far West became increasingly apparent. And Mr Sutter went bankrupt.

The real history of California was just beginning: in 1850 the United States of America made the former Mexican territory the thirty-first state of the Union. It was a bizarre situation. The laws of Mexico, the old mother country, no longer applied, and there was as yet no state parliament to pass new ones. More than 80,000 prospectors swarmed into the state. The sheriff's tin star counted for little; there were shootings and lynchings, and many a 'forty-niner' was proved innocent only after he had already been hanged.

And then, miraculously, this society of scoundrels, desperados, whores, drunks and speculators changed, reformed, began building churches and opera houses, married into the local population and shrewdly invested the gold discovered in the wild years. Cities were founded, Sacramento became the state capital and a parliament was elected. The foundations of California, America's Golden State, had been laid.

California's Indian past

5,000 years ago Indian nomads roamed the plains of California; they were isolated tribes, whose forefathers had arrived from Asia, via the Aleutian Islands, more than 70,000 years before. While the tribes in the Great Plains enjoyed rich hunting grounds, those on the coast and in the desert regions concentrated on gathering roots and catching small animals. For a long time the Indians – more than 300 tribes – had the territory to themselves, until they were decimated by the invasion of white settlers, particularly at the time of the 1849 Gold Rush. The oldest remains of California's Indian past are scarcely more than 1,000 years old.

How California got its name

The first Spaniards arrived in 1542, sailing northwards from their Mexican colony along the Pacific coast. They had no inkling of California's gold reserves, and do not seem to have been inclined to take possession of the forbidding steep coast. The captain of this first voyage was Juan Rodriguez Cabrillo, a Portuguese in the service of Spain.

The Spaniards needed a name for this region, and California was christened in a quite extraordinary way. Cabrillo remembered the story 'Las Sergas de Esplandián', published in 1510 by the Spanish writer Montalvo, which describes an island close to Paradise, inhabited by beautiful, naked but warlike women and rich in gold and precious stones. It was called California. California! And so an imaginary and fantastical island inspired the name of the future gold state of California.

The English interlude

In 1579 Sir Francis Drake landed in San Francisco Bay and annexed the territory for England. However, none of his countrymen followed him, and his discovery was forgotten. The native Indians continued to fish peacefully, to weave baskets and dig up roots. For more than 100 years they were undisturbed by white people.

California's conquest by the whites

Eventually men of religion appeared and conquered California for the white races: Jesuits, Franciscans and finally Dominicans turned the Indians away from their gods of thunder and instilled Christianity in them. Between 1769 and 1823 they built, from stone or clay bricks, a total of twenty-one missions dedicated to their familiar saints, San Diego, San Carlos, San Antonio, San Gabriel. A thoroughly efficient communications network thus arose. The King of Spain was delighted to hear of it, and allowed the chain of Spanish missions in the far west of America to be called *El camino real*, the royal highway. With good reason: the Franciscan missions spread not only the word of God, but Spanish culture as well. The *padres* read mass, bound wounds, taught Indians to read and write, explored the hinterland, bred cattle and pigs and showed the Indians how to use a plough, to tan leather, to irrigate fields and to cultivate trees. The missions developed into massive estates, with 31,000 Indian workers.

The Russians come – and go

The Spanish viceroy in Mexico sent soldiers after the missionaries, for reasons of security. Foreigners often appeared along the coast, among them Russian fur-hunters who had come across from Siberia. In 1812 they settled in the new hunting regions and founded a trading post, Fort Ross. But their plans were not fulfilled. In 1841, after less than thirty years in California, they sold their base to John Sutter. The Russian Orthodox chapel has been restored and is now open to visitors. Russian Hill in San Francisco is a reminder of the brief presence of Russian hunters and traders on the American continent.

California's independence

By this time, California had got into an awkward, complicated situation. Mexico to the south declared its independence from Spain in 1821. The United States obviously had designs on the Pacific coast. The missions were taken away from the Church, as were the monasteries in Napoleonic Europe. Quick-thinking Californian families took possession of the massive estates and the 750,000 cattle belonging to the Franciscan *padres*. Suddenly there was talk of an independent California – independent of Mexico, which ought to be sympathetic because of its own recent declaration of independence. In the distance shots were already being fired.

The American captain T. A. C. Jones was cruising off Monterey, bent on a display of heroism. Scouts were whispering of English warships. There were rumours of war between the USA and Mexico. The captain gave the signal to attack: the bewildered Monterey garrison surrendered without firing a shot. The delighted captain had the US flag hoisted over the town. It did not flutter there for long: the captain had made a mistake. There was no war, no English fleet. The Stars and Stripes was hauled down, the captain said to his Mexican colleagues, 'No hard feelings,' and sailed off, a Charlie Chaplin of naval warfare history.

However, trouble was brewing. Intrigues were being hatched. The Americans were speaking quite openly of annexation. A Californian flag was designed, with a bear in the centre field. It is still the official flag of the state of California.

War between the USA and Mexico could not be avoided; it began in 1846, and California was really only a secondary issue. There was no fighting in California, apart from an engagement near San Pasqual, in which twenty-two people died – the bloodiest conflict in the history of California, and one that marked the end of the state's military history. In 1848, in the Treaty of Guadalupe Hidalgo, Mexico reluctantly ceded California, an area of 158,706 sq miles (411,047 sq km), to the USA.

California has only once been directly confronted with world history, and even then only incidentally: on June 26th 1945, fifty-one nations signed the United Nations Charter in the San Francisco Opera House.

Windsurfing, San Diego

⚡ First and foremost: recreation

If California were to be characterised in catchwords, *recreation* would be at the top of the list. That is: recuperation, relaxation, amusement, sport, invigoration. California is a Mecca for holidaymakers.

However, just in case you are expecting things that are better sought elsewhere, it is as well to mention at the outset a few things you will *not* find in California. There is little art to be seen, except of course in the large museums and galleries in the three metropolises of Los Angeles, San Francisco and San Diego. It is not a land of milk and honey, like France for example. However, although there are few atmospheric bars, the quality of the food is thoroughly reliable, and fish and seafood are to be especially recommended. It is a state for car-drivers. The landscapes between the Sierra and the Pacific are magnificent, primeval, ghostly – but certainly not charming.

California is for lovers of sport. *Watersports* take first place in southern California, although the north can boast *Lake Tahoe*. Swimming, surfing and deep-sea fishing are in season all year round in the south. If the very active environmental movement does not intervene, *dune-bugging*, the daredevil cross-country motor races featuring souped-up motor bikes and convertibles equipped with special tyres, is expected to become more popular. The triumphal progress of the *hang-gliders* began on the Pacific coast in California: most of the international masters of this extraordinary sport come from here. *White-water rafting*, an adventurous watersport, has quickly become fashionable on the torrential rivers of the Sierra Nevada – the Klamath, the American River and the Eel River; special rubber rafts for tourists are available in the summer. Those who prefer to remain on less turbulent water will find themselves well served by the many artificial lakes; there are more than a hundred, most of them accessible to boats, swimmers and anglers.

Yes, anglers! In no other state are there so many passionate anglers as in California, with its foaming, ice-cold mountain streams and numerous dark lakes

*El Capitan,
Yosemite*

which harbour salmon, perch, catfish and many different species of trout. Fishing licences can be bought quite easily.

Outdoors is one of the key words in any understanding of California. Outdoor activities include the daunting climb up the vertical granite cliffs of *El Capitan* in *Yosemite* as well as trips through the green shade of *Sequoia National Park*. Those who like walking will find virtually infinite scope on the *Pacific Crest Trail*, the footpath that will one day run the full length of California from north to south, a distance of more than 800 miles (1,300 km).

And although California is the most populous state of the Union, highly civilised, heavily motorised, as developed as possible and covered by a dense network of first-class roads, most of it is still wilderness. If you want to experience this at first hand, you should obtain a *wilderness permit*, a document which may at first seem a rather odd paradox. You should present it at the entrance to one of the large national or state parks and give your planned time of return. If this deadline is significantly exceeded, the park authorities will know that search parties should be mobilised.

Golf has long been a people's sport in the USA; there is enough space for golf courses in virtually every sizeable place. The same is true of *tennis courts* and *swimming pools*, particularly in the south. The latest development is *mineral pools*, swimming pools containing effervescent mineral water from natural springs rather than ordinary, over-chlorinated mains water. Another popular activity is *dude ranching*: horseback excursions from ranches that have been converted into hotels and which provide their guests with horses, guides, broad-brimmed cowboy hats and trips into the Wild West, including steaks for the camp-fire and a coyote in the distance. (Detailed information about outdoor holidays, with lists of addresses, can be obtained from *Adventure Guides*, 36 East 57 St, New York, NY 10022; ask for the brochure *Adventure Travel, USA*.)

Among the Californian *winter sports* centres, there is one with a world-wide reputation: *Squaw Valley*, site of the 1960 Winter Olympics, where the ski-lifts are in operation all year round. Squaw Valley is conveniently situated close to the somewhat overcrowded holiday area around Lake Tahoe, four hours by car north-east of San Francisco. Winter sports resorts continue to be developed in the foothills of the Sierra Nevada — on Silver Lake, above Pinecrest Lake, in Kings Canyon National Park and in the hinterland to the east of Los Angeles. The USA has long been a nation of skiers.

Autumn marks the start of the *football* season, American football, that is, in which giants of men with their rectangular padded shoulders fight with ruthless aggression for possession of an oval piece of leather. The game non-Americans know as football is called *soccer* here, and is gaining in popularity. It is worth while trying to see one of the major *baseball* finals, even if you do not fully understand the complicated rules, but these are often hopelessly sold out.

From San Diego it is only a stone's throw to *Tijuana*, the Mexican border town, which used to have an extremely dubious reputation. *Bullfights* are held here, and even attract star toreadors from Spain. And in smaller towns and on fairgrounds you can watch a *rodeo*.

Bears, whales, hummingbirds and sequoias

In *Yosemite National Park* and in many other densely forested mountain regions you must be ready to brake sharply if a brownish-black bear suddenly appears from the undergrowth and ambles across the road. This is such a common occurrence that the bear has become California's heraldic animal. *Take care*. Do not feed bears and do not stroke them; stay in your car. If you are lucky, you may see the rare giant of the western skies, the Californian condor, in *Los Padres National Forest*. On the other hand, the smallest of all masters of flight, the hummingbird, is by no means a rarity. These miraculous tiny birds, which can hover virtually motionless in the air like helicopters, are often pampered with hanging baskets containing honey-filled plastic flowers. The smallest hummingbirds weigh only two grams, but each one takes in four times its body weight of nectar every day — fuel for flight muscles, which can beat up to an incredible eighty times per second.

California is one enormous open-air wildlife park. Thousands of sea-lions shuffle around below the cliffs of the islands near San Francisco and on the Channel Islands off Santa Barbara. The grey whale, now almost extinct, comes close to the coast, and flocks of pelicans and cormorants waddle on the cliff ledges. In the Sierras wildcats are common.

Other Californian favourites are the restless ground squirrel, the voracious grey squirrel ('tree rat' might be a more appropriate name) and the elegant tufted quail. There are also beavers, grey foxes and coyotes. If in the evening you suddenly become aware of a strong smell of burning rubber that does not fade even after you have driven several hundred yards, then you have passed a skunk, an animal the size of a cat which is capable of spraying its evil-smelling fluid in a well-directed jet for a distance of about four yards — woe betide anyone who gets in the way!

California's most celebrated plant is known as the *General Sherman Tree* and is in the Giant Forest of Sequoia National Park, 2½ hours' drive north of Los Angeles. It is a massive tree of the *Sequoia gigantea* family, commonly known as the giant sequoia. The 'General' is 275 ft (83.8 m) in height and probably 3,500 years old. It is named after General William Tecumseh Sherman, who in 1864 made a decisive contribution to the Union victory in the American Civil War.

The sequoias and their brothers the redwoods (*Sequoia sempervirens*) are the botanical pride of California, curiosities to be protected. The redwoods, with their

massive trunks thrusting ramrod-straight towards the sky, have been growing near the coast for 30 million years; some of them are 400 ft (122 m) high! Time has no meaning for them. But if *you* are in a hurry, then drive from San Francisco to *Muir Woods National Monument*, just 20 miles (30 km) north of the Golden Gate Bridge, although the redwoods here are only 240 ft (73 m) high.

Before you take the wheel – a note for visitors from overseas

The road network here is first class. The superhighways, America's multi-lane version of the European motorways, run in almost straight lines between the major cities. Californian motorists are polite, helpful and relaxed. Even the state highways are in excellent condition. In contrast to the situation in the east-coast states, there are no tolls on California's highways.

Since the oil crisis of the 1970s, the speed limit in all states of the USA has been 55 mph (88 kph). This speed limit applies to all roads – superhighways, interstate, federal, state – everywhere, unless an even lower limit is indicated by white signs, or unless (in the case of certain highways running through thinly settled areas) a limit of 65 mph is clearly marked. Infringements of the speed limits are reported by the American police – and fines are collected by magistrates with powers of summary jurisdiction. If you find yourself being followed by the police because you have not yet adjusted to the slower pace of driving in California, you should pull in to the right (the side, of course, on which Americans drive) and stop the car, but *don't* get out. The police officer will come to you. After a while you will perhaps learn to appreciate the lack of stress when travelling on California's roads.

American lorries (trucks) travel as quickly as cars. They also operate at weekends. There is much less overtaking than on European roads. On multi-lane highways, all two, three or four lanes have equal status. Since all traffic travels at more or less the same slowish pace, the distance between two places in the USA is often given in hours, even on road maps. Of course these times do not apply to long holiday weekends, when most of California's 12 million (!) cars are on the road. In an attempt to prevent this enormous stream of traffic from coming to a halt, Californian law forbids you to allow your car to run out of fuel, and not only on the highways.

The steep roller-coaster roads of San Francisco require an additional precaution: when you park your car, you must turn the front wheels at an angle to the kerb, in order that it cannot under any circumstances roll downhill. Turn them inwards when you face downhill, and outwards when you face uphill. This practice is law in San Francisco.

American road signs are easy to understand. The major roads are numbered, and exits from highways are also numbered. They are announced in good time, but the last sign is located after the exit. Large and medium-sized towns always have several exits which, to the confusion of strangers, bear the names of adjoining streets. You are recommended to purchase the *Rand McNally Road Atlas*, a new edition of which is published each year.

Left: One of California's massive redwood trees

⚔ Visitors' guide to food and drink in California

Before the man was brought to the gallows, the sheriff's assistant asked him whether he would like anything to eat. Of course, said the man, hanging makes you hungry. And so he ordered an omelette with strips of ham and oysters. This Californian delicacy is aptly called the *Hangtown Fry*, in memory of its inventor, and is still served in Maye's Oyster House in San Francisco, where the moving story is also preserved.

Californian food may not be particularly distinctive, but the portions are certainly ample, sufficient indeed to satisfy the appetites of lumberjacks. Recipes are simple. The long coastline means there is a plentiful supply of first-class fish, crawfish, prawns (called shrimp in America), crabs and oysters, as well as many types of mussels and other shellfish. The enormous farms in the Central Valley supply fresh fruit and vegetables. In addition, California is one of the strongholds of the health food movement. Spanish-Mexican and Chinese food are already a traditional part of Californian cuisine, and Japanese *sushi bars* have recently become fashionable.

Steak: America's favourite meal

The meat is almost always of top quality. Because all parts of the cow are used to produce steaks in America, restaurant menus list a confusing proliferation of different cuts. *Porterhouse steaks* hang over the edge of the plate, and are sufficient to feed a whole family. The best steak is said to be the *filet mignon*, a fillet steak two fingers thick, encased in bacon. *Round steak* is cut from the leg, *sirloin* from the hip; *rib steak* comes of course from the ribs, while *brisket* is an excellent cut from the shoulder, tender and aromatic. Cooks in America also cut steaks from salmon, halibut and turkey.

Steak is handled with care, and the waiter will ask you how you want it cooked. You have six options, ranging from rare through medium rare, medium, medium done and done to well done.

America's favourite meal

Finger food

Finger food was invented in America. This fast, cheap kind of food is typified by the hamburger, the ubiquitous round of unseasoned minced meat, served in a white bread roll, made palatable with mayonnaise, ketchup, pickled gherkins, onions and lettuce leaves and supplemented by a serving of French fries.

Sandwiches, of course, also belong in the category of finger food. They can be filled with ham, Swiss cheese (Emmental type) or American cheese (golden-yellow, mild cheese of the Cheddar type), liver sausage, salami, egg mayonnaise or tuna fish, served in white bread or rye bread with caraway seeds, in rolls or French sticks, and toasted if requested.

Two original sandwich recipes:

The BLT: bacon, lettuce and tomato, with both pieces of bread spread with butter or mayonnaise.

The submarine: a combination of cheese and sausage (two sorts of each), highly spiced and stuffed, together with lettuce leaves, into half a French stick. Must be held in both hands!

Apple pie

Curiously enough, it is a sweet dish that rates as the most American of all American specialities – 'as American as apple pie' is a stock saying. American apple pies are usually quite strongly flavoured with cinnamon and mace, and if you order *apple pie à la mode* it will be served with vanilla ice-cream.

Foreign cuisines on the menu

The proximity of Mexico and the stream of Mexican immigrants has had a significant influence on Californian food. The commonest dish is the spicy, poor man's fare *chilli con carne*, a bean stew made with minced meat and flavoured with chilli powder, which in American fast-food kitchens unfortunately loses its original pungency. Many variations on the basic *tortilla* are available, and in the evening Mexican beer (*cerveza*) will wash them down very nicely. In southern California *enchiladas* (spicy cornmeal pancakes filled with meat) are as common as hamburgers.

The American tradition of cooking has its origins in England, but many Californian cooks are Italian or Chinese. In the Chinatowns of both San Francisco and Los Angeles there are innumerable restaurants. You can even choose from several different regional cuisines. Many Chinese restaurants do not serve alcohol, but they all serve tea. Other Asian cuisines can also be sampled, including Japanese, Korean and Vietnamese.

Breakfast – lunch – dinner

Unless you are travelling with a tour operator who arranges everything for you, the cost of your hotel room does *not* include breakfast. You can have breakfast either in the hotel coffee-shop or in a nearby eating place, where you sit either at the counter or at one of the small tables.

The glorious American breakfast begins with orange-juice (in good restaurants this is freshly squeezed and is almost always better than what goes under the same name in Europe) and/or cereal. Boiled eggs are virtually unknown, because they have to be prepared individually, which takes too long. The waiter will ask you how you want your eggs: fried, poached, scrambled or in an omelette. With fried eggs you have a choice between *sunny side up* (fried on one side only) and *over* (fried on both sides so that the yolk hardens), and between *medium* and *well done*. To accompany your eggs you can have bacon, ham or sausages. In addition, Californian eating places spoil their customers with *hash browns* (fried potato cakes).

Luncheonettes are snack bars that serve lunches. *Cafeterias* are self-service restaurants, usually open all day, where there is no need to tip. In all other restaurants you should reckon on a 15–20% service charge or tip.

Dinner is usually more expensive than lunch. A *lobster Newburg* (lobster stew with cream and sherry) which costs $12 at lunch-time may figure on the evening menu at $15.50 for the same portion. If you are ravenously hungry and do not constantly have to count the quarters in your purse, you will do better with the more expensive 'complete dinner' than the *à la carte* menu.

There is one strictly observed convention in America, which is otherwise so casual: on entering a restaurant you should wait until the 'hostess' greets you with an armful of menus and shows you to a table. You do not sit down at tables already occupied by other diners, even if there are empty chairs. Smart restaurants require male diners to wear jacket and tie. Alcoholic drinks are served only to those over twenty-one years of age; waiting-staff risk immediate dismissal and the owner the loss of his licence if this strictly enforced law is infringed.

Drinks

America is very proud of its coffee. Refills are usually free, and you can often have as many as you wish. Beer is usually brought to your table in a bottle or can, but always so ice-cold that no real head can form in the glass. If you order beer, the waiter will ask you which brand you want: *Miller's, Budweiser (Bud), Schlitz* and *Coors* are some of the favourites. They are all very similar: light, Pilsner-type beers, slightly less strongly flavoured than some European varieties. Americans also have a great thirst for imported beers from Holland, Denmark and Germany; these must, however, be brewed to meet the American preference for a lower alcohol content than that of the European equivalents. Draught beer is also very popular in America, and some resourceful brewers have even hit upon the rather surprising idea of producing draught beer in cans!

Cheers!

Napa Valley – California's main wine-producing area

Three cheers for Californian wine!

It has always been known that wine is produced near the Pacific. Nobody took it seriously: how could decent wine be made in the country that invented Coca-Cola and sickly sweet milk shakes? But then came the great bombshell – and all of a sudden, with one brilliant advertising coup, Californian wine was world famous. The year was 1976.

In horrified tones, and yet with an undercurrent of spiteful glee, the newspapers reported that a wine-dealer in Paris had convened a jury of respected wine-tasters and had presented them with a range of fine wines to sample. When the sensitive jurors had delivered their verdicts and ranked the wines they had tasted, the host disclosed such an outrageous secret that the jurors almost fell off their chairs: first and third places had been given to wines from California, which had also taken fifth and sixth positions. Ever since then, wine buffs have had to add a few new valleys to their list, particularly the *Napa Valley* (see page 45), the *San Joaquin Valley* to the south-east and the area around Salinas.

What is this wine like? Not cheap, but good value for money, reliable and clean. The top names are outstanding, while the mass-produced wines are very respectable. The Californian wine industry is based on the cultivation of European grape varieties. The climate and soils are ideal, although there are obviously tremendous differences between *Sonoma County*, close to the coast, and *Bakersfield*, at the foot of the *Sierra Nevada*. The Pacific fog sweeps over the vineyards along the *Russian River*, while in the windless, dry heat of the flatlands of the *Central Valley* grapes of extravagant sweetness are grown, which are cooled down by sprays of artificial mist. Californian still wines are first class, and the sparkling wines are of high quality.

One of the great pleasures of a journey through California is to stop at a supermarket, purchase a chilled bottle of light white wine, a French stick, some salami, a piece of cheese and some fresh fruit, and then find a shady spot in the countryside for a picnic.

Don't forget your fig-leaf!

For many years the night sky of Los Angeles was pierced by the pencil beam of an old anti-aircraft searchlight. Connoisseurs knew that next to the beam stood the bar in which America's most vulgar striptease shows were presented. A policeman in uniform always stood at the entrance. When the American rebellion against prudery first began, support for the new freedoms was particularly strong in California.

San Francisco has a reputation as a liberal haven for sexual minorities. When the great gay summer parade offers pantomime and cabaret to the public gaze, the law does not intervene. As recently as 1980, however, a Californian court banned nude bathing on beaches. Nevertheless there are several naturist areas: near *La Jolla* (San Diego), *Laguna Beach*, *Santa Barbara* and *Leo Carillo State Beach* (on Highway 1 between *Santa Monica* and *Ventura*). In the official naturist areas even the police have no objection to nude bathers. Here they are called *sunbathers*. If you want to know exactly where you can leave all your clothes behind, write to the *American Sunbathing Association*, 810 North Millo, Orlando, Fla. They will send you addresses and regulations.

Where to stay

You are unlikely to make a real mistake with hotels in California. Most accommodation – from de luxe hotels to remote motels – is clean, practical and air-conditioned, with a private bath or shower, a toilet and a colour television set. There is often a swimming pool, either adjoining the hotel or on the roof.

Because of the recent massive increase in the number of people leaving without paying their bills, hotels usually request new arrivals to pay in advance. There is one exception to this: if you have an internationally recognised credit card, the hotel will simply take a copy of it as a precaution.

Foreign visitors will never be asked to surrender their passports. Some hotels

Roadside motels . . .

. . . and seaside apartments

require you to pay a modest deposit for your room key. This is because in American hotels keys are not left at reception but kept by guests until they check out. In up-market hotels computerised cards have replaced keys. Unfortunately, hotels have become a magnet for thieves and other criminals: this is immediately apparent from the grotesqely elaborate security devices fixed to the doors. The hotel management will recommend that valuables be deposited in the hotel safe.

The various names for different kinds of accommodation in America can confuse a foreigner. *Hotel* is self-explanatory; a *motor hotel* is usually outside the city centre, with sufficient parking space and almost always a swimming pool. *Motels* are also geared to the needs of motorists, with a parking place in front of the door to each room, but no restaurant. *Motor inns* are generally larger and more luxurious, usually with a coffee-shop or a snack bar, sufficient parking space, of course, and often a swimming pool. The term *lodge* indicates a rural atmosphere in a holiday region, usually with individual chalets, car-parks and a restaurant. *Resorts* are never in towns or cities, but in mountains, on beaches or beside lakes; they have a swimming pool, boating, tennis courts or golf course and a restaurant, and sometimes offer half board (*American plan*). Finally, there is one other type of accommodation that is typical of the south and south-west of the USA: the *ranch*. In addition to the usual accommodation, ranches always offer particular leisure activities, usually horse-riding, but also golf, tennis and guided excursions into the picturesque surroundings.

Reliable, low-cost accommodation is still offered by the 'Ys', the common American abbreviation for the YMCA and YWCA, in simple but clean hostels, usually in city centres. Rooms here cost about half as much as in comparable hotels. There is usually separate accommodation for men and women, although couples are also accepted in the bigger cities. Reservation well in advance is recommended. Further information can be obtained from the *National Council of the YMCA,* 291 Broadway, New York, NY 10007.

Hints for your holiday

California has rarely had difficulties accommodating foreigners – ever since the legendary Gold Rush of 1849 it has always been the favourite destination of immigrants from both within and outside the USA. As soon as you arrive, you will become aware of the easy-going atmosphere. The only rules you need observe are those that apply universally to guests: be polite and friendly. Fun is a favourite word in the Californian vocabulary, so – have fun!

Old Sacramento Candy Barrel Store

Where to go and what to see

San Francisco skyline

San Francisco

San Francisco is spread over about forty hills and lies at the northern tip of the peninsula between the Pacific Ocean and San Francisco Bay. The entrance to the Bay, which is nearly a mile (1,400 m) wide, is known as the Golden Gate and is spanned by the celebrated *Golden Gate Bridge*.

The city has a population of 743,000 and cannot therefore compete with those US metropolises that count their populations in millions, although more than three million people live in the metropolitan area. Nevertheless, the city can boast the headquarters of the *Bank of America*, the largest bank in the world, and its Financial District is a very important business centre. San Francisco's Chinatown is the largest Chinese quarter outside Asia. There are also wharfs, a large meat industry, fishing fleets and sugar refineries. With its *cable cars* on the one hand and the *Bay Area Rapid Transit* (BART) system on the other, the city has both one of the most antiquated and one of the most modern urban transport systems in the USA. And it is known as one of the most beautiful cities in North America.

Rudyard Kipling was both repelled and fascinated by the place, describing it as 'a mad city, inhabited for the most part by perfectly insane people'. The city's inhabitants are fond of quoting him: crazy people and crazy ideas are part of the city. And even if the conflicts are sometimes intense, San Francisco is a liberal city. The hippy movement started here. People in San Francisco are more tolerant than elsewhere towards minorities, such as homosexuals, and so the city has become a magnet for them. (Despite the liberal attitudes of most of the population, tensions have been growing since the appearance of Aids.)

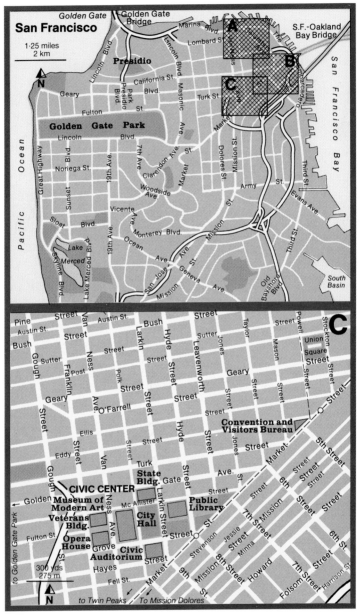

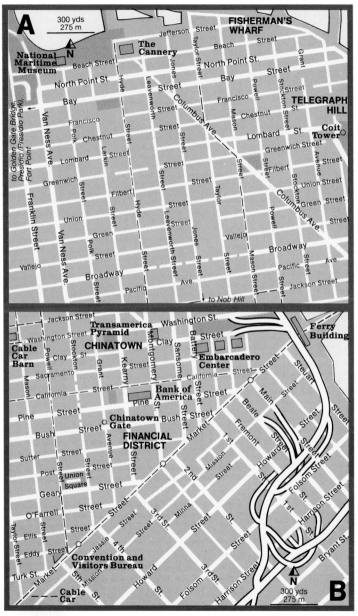

A

300 yds
275 m

N

FISHERMAN'S WHARF

National Maritime Museum

The Cannery

Jefferson Street
Beach Street
North Point St.
Bay Street
Francisco Street
Chestnut Street

Beach Street
North Point St.
Bay Street

Grant Street
Stockton Street

TELEGRAPH HILL

Beach Street
North Point St.
Bay
Francisco
Chestnut
Lombard St.

Greenwich Street

Coit Tower

to Golden Gate Bridge, Presidio (Presidio Park), Fort Point

Van Ness Ave.
Franklin Street
Polk Street
Larkin Street
Hyde Street
Leavenworth Street
Columbus Ave.

North Point St.
Bay
Francisco
Chestnut
Lombard
Greenwich
Filbert Street
Union Street
Green Street
Broadway
Pacific

Taylor
Jones Street
Mason Street
Powell
Stockton
Avenue
Columbus Ave.

Filbert Street
Union Street
Green
Street

Vallejo
Broadway
Pacific
Jackson Street

↓ to Nob Hill

B

Jackson Street
Washington Street
Transamerica Pyramid
Washington St.

Ferry Building

Cable Car Barn

CHINATOWN

Powell
Mason
Stockton St.
Clay
Sacramento
California
Grant
Kearny
Montgomery
Clay Street
Pine

California Street

Battery Street
Sansome

Embarcadero Center

California Street
Pine Street
Bush Street

Bank of America

Chinatown Gate

FINANCIAL DISTRICT

Pine Street
Bush
Sutter
Post Street
Geary Street
O'Farrell Street
Ellis Street
Eddy Street
Turk St.

Grant Avenue
Stockton Street

Union Square

Market Street

Market Street
Mission Street
2nd
3rd St.
Minna
4th Street
Jessie
5th St.
Mission St.
Howard

Beale
Fremont
1st
Howard
Folsom Street
Harrison Street

Main Street
Steuart Street
Street
1st St.
Folsom Street
Harrison Street
Bryant St.

Convention and Visitors Bureau

Cable Car

N

300 yds
275 m

Those who are sound of wind and limb are in luck: this is a city for walkers, preferably hill-walkers. The streets really are as steep as they look in the cinema and on television. The cable cars clatter up and down the hills – they are almost always overcrowded, and are romantic relics rather than practical means of transport. But they *always* have priority!

Although many of the sights can be reached on foot, a drive by car through the city can also be recommended: follow the square blue and white signs. They bear a seagull's head and guide the tourist through the whole city, from the Civic Center (see page 30), over the most famous hills to the bustling Fisherman's Wharf (see page 30) and the Golden Gate Bridge, through parks and residential streets with narrow Late Victorian houses to Seal Rock, with its bobbing, waddling, screeching population of sea-lions and sea-birds. The route is 49 miles (79 km) long, and is known as the *49 Miles Scenic Drive*. The signs constantly seem to be disappearing, but then the seagull's head suddenly pops up again. The whole trip takes almost a day to complete. Maps can be obtained free of charge from hotels, filling stations and restaurants – and, of course, from a place you should visit on your first day: the *Convention and Visitors Bureau*, 900 Market St, the city tourist office (Hallidie Plaza, tel. 415 974 6900). Here you can obtain information about the city, maps, calendars of events, weekly reviews, timetables and up-to-date price lists. And when you emerge from the basement back on to Market Street, you can join the queue of people round the corner waiting patiently for the cable car. It is worth while riding the cable car from Powell Street to the harbour. Immediately after Union Square, the business centre of the city, the cable car begins to climb

steeply up to *Nob Hill* (see page 33). It then grinds its way down to the harbour, with right-angle bends, agitated ringing of its bell and a final downhill run taken in stages.

The cable cars are technical dinosaurs. An endless cable runs through a trench beneath the tracks at a speed of about 12 mph (nearly 20 kph). When he wants to start the car, the driver, known as the *gripman*, catches hold of the steel cable with a grip that works like a pair of pliers. As soon as he releases the cable, the car comes to a halt. The people of San Francisco are very fond of the ancient, open, overcrowded veterans. The city authorities were going to get rid of the cable cars – but a determined campaign prevented them from doing so. The three remaining lines have since been placed under a preservation order.

Journeys by cable car are fairly cheap, and transfers are free. The cars are part of the Municipal Railways system, known as MUNI. The system also includes trolley cars and buses and provides access to all the city's sights. Sundays and public holidays are good days to try it out, since you can then buy a special ticket enabling you to travel all day on all parts of the MUNI system. The futuristic BART system, installed at a cost of many millions of dollars, links San Francisco to the cities on the other side of the Bay and is an attraction in itself.

A city whose unique character is determined by its position on, in and above water deserves to be viewed from a ship. *Golden Gate Ferries* (which depart from the end of Market Street, near the old, imposing *Ferry Building*) will take you across the Bay to *Sausalito* (Red and White Fleet from Pier 41) and *Richmond*. As you cross the Bay, a magnificent panorama will unfurl on all sides

– the city with the unmistakable Transamerica Pyramid, the sweep of the *Bay Bridge* (see page 28), and in the opposite direction the flawless elegance of the *Golden Gate Bridge* (see page 32) and a brief glimpse of the open Pacific, the hills, the islands and the cities of Oakland and Richmond.

Of course there are also sightseeing tours by boat (from Piers 39 and 45) or a trip across to the notorious prison island of *Alcatraz* (see page 28). The most beautiful of the three islands in the Bay is Angel Island (Red and White Fleet from Pier 43½).

If you are a confirmed walker and want to get to know the city at first hand, you should ask in the Convention and Visitors Bureau (see page 26) for the latest list of walking tours. These tours, led by an expert, concentrate on particular districts of the city or on particular subjects. Examples include Chinatown (3 hours), architecture (4 hours), 'The Best of San Francisco' (5 hours) and a day's hiking through the vineyards of the Napa Valley, winetasting included.

You can have a lot of fun in San Francisco, even if you do not visit any of the obligatory sights. You can climb hills that immediately plunge precipitously down again, pause for breath at an amazing new view over the Pacific or the sharply etched silhouette of the city, stroll among the midday crowds in the glass canyons of the Financial District, go shivering into a smart shop in Union Square and buy a sweater to keep you warm in the summer chill, and wander through the leafy maze of the *Golden Gate Park* (see page 32). And in the evening you can drive over to *Sausalito* with the shimmering splendour of the Bay Area cities in front of you, dine on fish accompanied by Californian wine, make the acquaintance of some un-

San Francisco – typical street

usual characters, visit some atmospheric bars and streets, listen to some strange musical sounds and enjoy new smells and views.

If you really want to know what The City, as the locals call it, is most proud of, just choose whatever takes your fancy from the following selection of attractions. It does not matter how you go, whether according to a plan or with constant detours: the charm of San Francisco will make itself felt anyway, wherever you go. The city's constantly changing kaleidoscope will draw you into its spell.

Oakland Bay Bridge

 The main sights

Alcatraz

The rocky island in the Bay is famous for the fortress-like prison in which America held its worst criminals until Robert Kennedy, then Attorney-General, ordered its closure in 1963. The gangster Al Capone, the murderer 'Machine Gun' Kelly and the train robber Roy Gardner were all imprisoned here. The security arrangements were faultless: no prisoner ever escaped. The Lee Morris brothers made an attempt in 1962, but they probably drowned in the strong, ice-cold currents of the Bay. The grim island is so popular that the two-hour trip (from Pier 41) must be booked in advance (tel. 546 2800 and 2805). The favourite place with tourists in the dilapidated prison is Death Row, where prisoners condemned to death were held. The view of San Francisco from the prison walls is, ironically, quite superb.

Bay Bridge

Nobody calls it by its full name: the *San Francisco–Oakland Bay Bridge*. It was the dress rehearsal for the Golden Gate Bridge, which was built slightly later. Unfortunately you can't cross it on foot. It is 7½ miles (12 km) long, sweeps in a wide arc across the Bay and has two levels. The bridge is actually divided into two sections: the first stretches from San Francisco to the island of *Yerba Buena*, and the second continues to *Oakland*. Built between 1933 and 1936 at a cost of $70 million, the bridge was a decisive step in the development of the communities around the Bay into a single economic region. It was severely damaged in the 1989 earthquake. (A small toll is payable by traffic coming into San Francisco.)

Chinatown

Its 75,000 inhabitants make this the largest Chinese settlement outside Asia.

Still dominated by powerful clans, it is a district of antiquated workshops, small factories, numerous eating places, vegetable shops, herbalists, slaughterhouses and souvenir shops, as well as façades decorated in Chinese style, pagoda roofs, and orange ribbons from the last New Year's celebrations, with good wishes and ambiguous predictions printed on them. Chinatown is the district of San Francisco with the strongest sense of tradition. The dialect of the southern Chinese province of Kwangtung is still spoken here, the cooking is Cantonese and the customs of the old homeland are maintained.

Visitors usually enter through the exotic *Chinatown Gate* (Grant Ave and Bush St). Grant Avenue is lined with restaurants, offices, and shops crammed with art objects, jewellery and junk from the People's Republic of China, Taiwan and Hong Kong. If you turn into the narrow side-streets that lead off Grant Street, such as *Commercial Street*, you will encounter the everyday life of the district, shorn of the Oriental setting, grey rather than brightly coloured, dreary rather than smiling.

There are no major sights to see in Chinatown. Its attraction lies rather in the atmosphere of an exotic, almost impenetrable enclave. The earthquake and fire of 1906 destroyed the old Chinese quarter. The district was rebuilt quickly, without Chinese ornamentation; the decorations, like the pagoda roofs on the telephone boxes, were added later, for the benefit of tourists.

The Financial District, hungry for building land, is already eating away the eastern edge of Chinatown: *Portsmouth Square* is overshadowed by the concrete block of the Holiday Inn and undermined by a subterranean car-park. Nevertheless, the unassuming square is a centre of Chinese community life. In the morning, sporty types can be seen doing *Tai Chi Chuan* exercises; later, old Chinese men come along to play chess. *Kuomintang Headquarters* (844 Stockton St), founded by Sun Yat-sen, the first president of the Republic of China, was a highly charged political centre, and the Kuomintang still exerts considerable influence on the Chinese community in San Francisco. Diagonally opposite, at 843 Stockton, was the *Chinese Six Companies Headquarters*, an organisation which exerted even greater influence over the Chinese population of California. The 'Six Companies' represented six Chinese provinces and the organisation was originally an employment agency for Chinese workers, as well as a wealthy political pressure group of entrepreneurs and a sort of Chinese court, outside the American judicial system. The façade is decorated with dragons, dogs, birds and flowers. Further information about the history and life-style of the Chinese on the west coast of America can be found at the *Chinese Historical Society of America* (17 Adler Place).

Chinatown

Civic Center

This is said to be the finest civic centre in the United States. The *City Hall*, built in 1915 and vaguely reminiscent of St Peter's in Rome, has a dome higher than that of the Capitol in Washington. It is an imposing building that looks like a prize-winning examination entry on the subject of Renaissance architecture. It has Doric pillars and, right at the top of the dome, a lantern, which is lit when the city council is in session at night. European visitors like to make fun of America's fondness for architectural imitation in its public buildings and churches, yet historicism also dominated architecture in Europe around the turn of the century.

City Hall dominates the *Civic Center Plaza*: on the west side is the *Civic Auditorium*, on the east the *State Building* and the *Public Library*. Hidden by the bulk of City Hall is the famous *Opera House* (with the *Davies Symphony Hall*, the home of the symphony orchestra). It was here in the summer of 1945 that the United Nations Charter was signed, an event which signalled the official birth of the United Nations. Next to the Opera House are the *Veterans' Building* and the *Museum of Modern Art*, both built in the style of the Civic Center. The ultra-modern *Convention Center* was opened in 1982.

Ferry Building

The Ferry Building, a stately tower modelled on Seville Cathedral, was once San Francisco's most famous landmark. The railway terminus has always been over the Bay in Oakland, and before the great Bay Bridge was built more than 50 million passengers every year continued their journey by ferry, disembarking at the Ferry Building. In 1958 the ferry service was almost completely discontinued, and since then the old Ferry Building has been put to a variety of temporary uses, including service as the *World Trade Center*; it also houses a mineral exhibition (admission free). The few remaining ferry lines, such as the boats to Sausalito, are located at the southern end of the Ferry Building.

The *Embarcadero* is the wide, traffic-filled shore boulevard. *Embarcadero One* and *Embarcadero Two* are the office blocks behind the Ferry Building. Number two, the *Levi Strauss Building*, is the blue-jeans centre of the world. Levi Strauss, a native of Bavaria, made a fortune out of sewing hard-wearing canvas trousers during the Gold Rush. The *Embarcadero Center* is a pedestrian zone with hotels, shops, a grassy area, passageways and restaurants, dominated by the *Transamerica Pyramid*.

Fisherman's Wharf

The wharf is now an extensive tourist area, packed with seafood restaurants and fish stalls. Fresh crabs, shrimps and prawns are sold here straight from the pot, with French sticks and dry white wine from the Napa Valley to accompany them. There are also several old-established restaurants specialising in all sorts of seafood. Fisherman's Wharf is San Francisco's premier tourist attraction, although the actual fishing fleet now occupies only a small part of the wharf between Leavenworth Street and Jones Street, not much more than one block. The rest of the area is taken up by souvenir shops, a wax museum, bars and the sailing ship *Balclutha*, a real veteran of Christian seafaring built in 1886 (Pier 43½). *Pier 39* is modelled after those wide wooden piers along which the general public can walk a little way out to sea. It is lined with shops, bars and amusements.

The Cannery is also part of the Fisherman's Wharf area; this is a former can-

Ghirardelli Square

ning factory, built of brick in 1909. It has been completely rebuilt and given a new lease of life, not as a factory but as a labyrinth of courtyards, staircases, passageways and balconies, filled with boutiques and restaurants. The whole project is a witty and extraordinarily successful experiment with new forms of urban architecture. San Francisco's Cannery was the first of its kind, and has since been copied in many parts of the world.

Ghirardelli Square

This is not a square but a unique space,
comparable to the Cannery. Once it was occupied by an old chocolate factory, scheduled for demolition. Parts of the walls are still standing, but the rest of the space was transformed by the imagination of a group of architects into an intricate, original urban landscape. Here you can stroll, go shopping, wander through galleries, try on a jacket, eat ice-cream or have dinner. There is an information desk that distributes maps of the complex. It is a modern bazaar, dominated by the clock tower and the enormous 'Ghirardelli' sign.

Traffic crossing Golden Gate Bridge

Golden Gate Bridge

Perhaps it is indeed the most beautiful bridge in the world, 1¾ miles (2.8 km) long, with a clear span of 1,400 yards (1,280 m) – dimensions which have long since been exceeded by other structures. Nevertheless, the Golden Gate Bridge is unique and unsurpassed, a perfect combination of technology, landscape and architecture. There were violent protests against its construction, on the grounds that it was technically impossible and that it would disfigure the *Golden Gate* (named, incidentally, after another spectacular strait, the Golden Horn in Istanbul). This is nonsense: the bridge has long been one of the wonders of the modern world. It is an engineering masterpiece, constructed by the bridge-builder J. B. Strauss between 1933 and 1937; it links the San Francisco peninsula with *Marin County*. It spans the Golden Gate less than 2 miles (3 km) before the point at which the strait suddenly opens out into the Pacific Ocean. From a distance the bridge looks like a pattern of delicate filigree work, but as you drive over its six-lane roadway the geometrical lattice-work of its 'strings' grows into a wire harp of superhuman dimensions. Tolls are paid only by traffic driving into the city. The bridge can be crossed on foot: an unforgettable walk with constantly changing panoramas. The water is so far below that ocean-going ships passing under the bridge look like toys. On the northern slope there are two viewpoints offering wonderful panoramas over the bridge, the city and the Bay.

Golden Gate Park

You can cross the park by car or by bicycle, on horseback or on foot. In any event, the trip will be packed with nature, art, amusement, sport and curiosities. The park covers an area of more than 1½ sq miles (412 ha), which makes it one-fifth bigger than Central Park in New York. It was infertile wasteland until it was turned into an artificial landscape with 5,000 different types of plants, a process that took thirty years. Now it has genuine Dutch *windmills* and century-old Australian eucalyptus trees, a dozen lakes and ponds, a golf course and a polo field, a buffalo herd, a *Botanical Garden* and a *Planetarium,* an auditorium for open-air concerts, a *Japanese Garden* with a tea-house, a strawberry island (*Strawberry Hill* in *Stow Lake*), lakes for model sailing-boats and fly-fishing, a rhododendron valley, rowing boats and motorboats, statues, bonsai trees and an enormous and immensely elaborate Late Victorian glass palace, the *Conservatory of Flowers*. And in the *De Young Memorial Museum* next to the open-air auditorium is the extraordinary collection of Oriental art treasures bequeathed by the multimillionaire Avery Brundage. The park is easily reached by public transport.

Mission Dolores

The Mission (Sixteenth and Dolores St) is not the towering basilica built in 1913, but the small building next to it with the gabled roof. It is San Francisco's oldest building, completed in 1791 (the year of Mozart's death). By the 1920s the old church was so dilapidated that it had to be practically rebuilt, with air-dried bricks made more durable by the addition of cement. Mission Dolores was in fact called *San Francisco de Asis*, after St Francis of Assisi. This name, in abbreviated form, has been retained as the name of the city but not, curiously enough, as that of its oldest church. The church is a textbook example of the so-called Mission style: a mixture of Spanish, Mexican, Baroque and rustic elements, snow-white exterior walls, fairly shallow-pitched roofs and stout beams, balconies, round arches and sturdy pillars. (Cinemas, department stores, stations, hotels and filling stations are also built in this style in California.) The Mission church, the original core of what was to become a world city, has a beautifully painted ceiling, a Spanish Baroque altar and a tabernacle from the Philippines, which also

belonged to Spain at the time it was built. Also of interest is the *cemetery*, with gravestones from the 19th c. – and a reminder of the 5,000 Indians who were converted to the new faith here, but died soon afterwards from diseases brought by the whites.

Nob Hill

The district was once so select that only children with governesses were allowed into *Huntington Park*, which lies at the top of the steep hill. San Francisco's élite, who had made their money from gold and silver, railways and stock exchange speculation, built their palaces here. The silver king 'Bonanza Jim' Fair built the *Fairmont* (950 Mason St), the city's most sumptuous luxury hotel. The great earthquake struck the day before it was due to be opened, and the Fairmont was gutted by fire. Fortunately it was built of the new reinforced concrete, so that all the walls remained standing, and it finally opened only a year late. To this day it remains one of the sights of San Francisco. Even if you are not staying there, go inside and walk sedately through the luxurious lobbies,

City Hall

Lombard Street – known as 'the crookedest street in the world'

bearing half left, until you come to the lift that will take you up the *Tower*. Get into the lift. Unlike most lifts, it does not hurtle skywards through a pitch-black shaft. The outer wall of the lift in the Fairmont Tower is made of glass, and as you glide slowly upwards it is an unforgettable experience to see the vista suddenly broaden out as cable cars and skyscrapers, bridges and ships come into view.

The equally famous *Mark Hopkins Hotel* (999 California St) has a Viennese coffee-house and a fascinating view, as well as a famous cocktail bar at the top of the building.

At the junction of *California* and *Powell Streets*, a supervisor in an observation tower prevents the cable cars from colliding as their paths cross at the intersection. It is a turbulent corner. Some of the architecture on Nob Hill is reminiscent of Florentine Renaissance and French Gothic styles, while the exclusive *Pacific Union Club* (1000 California St), built of brown sandstone, is

suggestive of a Late Roman villa. The building was completed in 1885, at the then incredible cost of $1,500,000; the sandstone was specially imported from New England. The expense was justified, for the building was the only private residence on Nob Hill that survived the earthquake of 1906. 'Snob Hill' is crowned by a devout copy: the Episcopal *Grace Cathedral* (California and Taylor Sts) is the Californian, reinforced-concrete version of Notre-Dame in Paris; the doors are copies of Ghiberti's Paradise Doors in Florence. Its carillon can be heard on Wednesdays and Sundays at 3 pm and 5 pm. Nob Hill is liveliest at lunch-time.

The Presidio

One of the Spanish words that is always cropping up in California: it means *fort*. The Presidio in San Francisco covers an area of 2.2 sq miles (580 ha) and, despite being used as army headquarters, looks like a park and is for the most part accessible without difficulty to civilians.

In 1776 the Spaniards built a fort at the entrance to the Bay. The approach road to the Golden Gate Bridge goes through the Presidio. Directly under the bridge, on the south bank, nestles the picturesque *Fort Point*, built in 1853 by the US army and closed down in 1914, since enemies were no longer expected here. In fact the guns guarding the Golden Gate never fired a shot in anger. During the construction of the bridge, which from down here looks like a gigantic space station, an extra arch was built over the fort. The site can be visited; friendly staff in Civil War uniforms explain the details. There are unusual views over the bridge, Bay and city.

Almost hidden in the depths of the Presidio are the headquarters of the US 6th Army, one of the oldest military support bases in the USA. The *Presidio Army Museum* can be visited free of charge (Lincoln Blvd and Funston Ave). All in all this must be the most relaxing military installation in America.

On the north-eastern edge of the Presidio is the curious *Palace of Fine Arts*. In 1915 a large Pan-Pacific exhibition was held in San Francisco to mark the opening of the Panama Canal; the Palace was built for the occasion – as a classical ruin. In 1958, when the 'ruin' was on the point of collapse, it was rebuilt and made more durable. (The restoration cost ten times more than the original building!) The building takes the form of an open circular temple, inspired by Arnold Böcklin's painting *The Island of the Dead*. It is a favourite with San Franciscans, particularly children, for it houses the *Exploratorium*, a hands-on science museum that seeks to explain physical phenomena with the aid of readily understandable working exhibits. It certainly makes a worthwhile detour (Baker St and Marina Blvd; accessible by public transport).

Telegraph Hill

Buses go up, there is even a car-park – but you should go up on foot, through *North Beach*, with its narrow wooden houses, the aroma of espresso, narrow cul-de-sacs, unashamedly vulgar dives, steep wooden steps, steep tracks overgrown with green and purple, elegant villas and modern studios. On the way you will see a hundred houses in any of which it would be nice to live for a year, and all different from each other. As you climb to the top of the hill, fresh views of other hills, of bridges and of water shimmer constantly through the luxuriant vegetation. There are no remarkable attractions except Telegraph Hill itself, a sought-after and very expensive residential district. Yet right at the top a world-famous landmark rises up from the hill, a tower of unmistakable singularity, really rather ugly, but a must for all visitors to San Francisco. Maybe it is true that it is modelled on a fire hose, since the 232-ft (71-m) *Coit Tower* (lift, admission charge) was built in 1934

Cable car

Transamerica Pyramid

with money bequeathed by Lillie Coit for the construction of a tower on Telegraph Hill as a memorial to firemen of San Francisco who had lost their lives. In order that the view of and from Coit Tower is not obstructed, the planning authorities do not permit the construction of high-rise buildings on Telegraph Hill. The view from the top is sensational.

The *pièce de résistance* in the tower itself is the frescos depicting aspects of Californian life, painted by twenty-five local artists. When the paintings were completed, there was an unprecedented scandal, and the city authorities temporarily closed the tower. The frescos, which were at once pamphlet and caricature, depiction and indictment of existing conditions, were politically too daring for the 1930s. Nobody was allowed to see them for four months, long enough for the most offensive sections to be painted over. Today, not even the names of the offended parties are known. Instead, visitors can become acquainted with the Mexican mural-painter Diego Rivera, who added to the frescos his own captivating motifs drawn from everyday life.

Transamerica Pyramid

It is most impressive when seen from a distance: extravagant, unmistakable, sumptuous, above all original. It dances above the boring skyscrapers in the Financial District that have accumulated over the past few decades like so many giant boxes, devoid of decoration or imagination. The Transamerica group (banking, insurance, haulage, private airline, real estate, computers, car rental) disregarded the logical but monotonous rule that, on exorbitantly expensive inner-city sites, the ground-plan of high-rise buildings must be followed all the way up to the roof, in order to ensure maximum use of space. Transamerica denied themselves hundreds of offices, for at the needle-point summit of their Pyramid there is no usable floor space. It is sheer luxury: 850 ft (260 m) high, 48 storeys, built in 1972 at a cost of $34 million – but with only about a third of the usable floor space of the Bank of America skyscraper built at about the same time. The unique silhouette forced the architects to develop new methods of equipping the Pyramid for everyday life. For example, the windows cannot be serviced by window-cleaners riding up and down the outer skin of the building in cages; instead, they are hinged in the middle and can be cleaned from the inside. And there was no room at the top of the Pyramid for the usual air-conditioning equipment, which had to be accommodated next to the building at ground level.

Four blocks away (California and Kearney Sts) is the tower of the *Bank of America* (which has its origins in San Francisco, was known as the Bank of Italy until 1930 and has a reputation as the 'little man's bank'). Only at first glance – and from a distance – is it just another high-rise box. It is 777 ft (237 m) high, has 52 storeys and was built in 1968. At close quarters, the elegant design of the reddish-brown granite giant becomes apparent: the façade, an artful arrangement of oriel windows, merges at street level into a lobby, in front of which a simple yet monumental plaza is spread like an expensive carpet.

The Financial District is known as the 'Wall Street of the West'. It is a series of steel and glass canyons, restaurants and shops, bars and, on the edges, nightclubs. At weekends it is quite deserted.

Twin Peaks

These two bald hills, 902 ft and 908 ft (275 and 277 m) high, can be reached by winding approach roads. On the hills themselves there is little to be seen except long terraces of family houses, but the view over the city and the *Bay Area* is uninterrupted in all directions. The Twin Peaks are favourite spots even at night-time: from nowhere else do the millions of lights on the far side of the Bay, between *Sausalito*, *Berkeley* and *San Lorenzo*, twinkle as captivatingly as from up here. The view can even be interesting in foggy weather, with the scene below constantly changing completely as the white clouds from the sea lie like gigantic fingers over parts of the city, while other districts bask in sunshine.

Union Square

This is the heart of the select business and hotel district in the city centre. In the middle is a park; around the edges are department stores, hotels, antique-

Union Square

shops, dazzlingly colourful flower stalls, palm trees – and roaring traffic. The quality of the architecture in Union Square cannot compare with that of Trafalgar Square or the Piazza Navona in Rome. However, the main square of San Francisco, which occupies a whole block and is dominated by billboards, is eagerly frequented by all sections of the population, from sunlovers relaxing during their lunch hour to diners arriving at the dignified *Grand Hotel St Francis*. Under the park is the first underground car-park to be built in the USA, opened in 1942; it goes down four storeys and has been copied in cities throughout the world. In the middle of the square is a column commemorating George Dewey's naval victory over the Spanish in Manila in 1898. The square is often the scene of demonstrations, and at Christmas, when the windows of the expensive stores are lit by colourful displays depicting the world of a remote American childhood, it shimmers like a huge Christmas tree. In the *Hyatt Hotel*

an original contemporary fountain plays; the wall around it depicts scenes from San Francisco life.

All these major attractions can be reached by public transport. A street map can be obtained free of charge from the *Visitors Information Center*, located in the basement of the Hallidie Plaza and accessible by escalator from Market Street. And although the city has a great many museums that are worth visiting (*Museum of Modern Art*, Civic Center, 401 Van Ness Ave; *Wells Fargo Museum*, 464 California St; *Cable Car Barn and Museum*, Washington and Mason Sts, depicting the history of the old cable cars; *S.F. Maritime Museum*, Aquatic Park on Polk St, and two dozen other art, science and historical museums), they are optional extras and never the real point of your journey.

Life-style

The real character of San Francisco lies in its location and its relaxed, civilised life-style, the highly individual Late

Victorian or modern terraced houses, each one noticeably different from its neighbour, the mixture of America, Europe and the Far East, the ghostly booming of foghorns, the aroma of air-dried salami, the snow-white dots of sailing boats in the Bay, an open-air jazz festival, dinner above the sea of lights, a Sunday morning in Little Italy or in the Mission District.

San Francisco is America's most popular city. Nobody calls it 'Frisco' – but 12,000 inhabitants know it as *Soko*; they are the Japanese of *Japantown* ('Nihomachi') and the endless flocks of tourists who fly over from Tokyo and who can eat and live as they do at home, for San Francisco has Japanese eating places on almost every corner. There are even more people of Italian descent – around 100,000 – so that home-made pasta can be bought all over the city.

The topless bar was invented in San Francisco, but has since disappeared. Most of the nightspots are located in the triangle bordered by Van Ness Avenue, Columbus Avenue and Market Street.

Cow Hollow was once a real pasture. It is now a smart shopping district covering eight blocks around Union Street: galleries, bars, boutiques, young people, and picturesque, turn-of-the-century houses, almost all with bay windows.

September and October are said to be the warmest months of the year, while January can be fairly cold. Even in summer, it is a good idea to keep a raincoat and a sweater to hand. At the many vantage-points and on the ferries it is almost always windy and cool. From the point of view of dress, San Francisco is more conservative than Los Angeles. Gentlemen with ties are less conspicuous than ladies in shorts.

 A look backwards

Compared with such ancient cities as Athens, Rome, London or Paris, San Francisco is still in its infancy. Three hundred years ago there was nothing here. Two hundred years ago a ship at last found the entrance to the bay, the largest natural harbour on the west coast of America. A hundred years ago the Gold Rush was over, and San Francisco had almost overnight been catapulted from a Spanish-Mexican mission village to its position as a rich city in the Wild West. California was now a separate state within the Union. The city on the bay grew at breakneck speed and a geometrical, right-angled street system was developed, with a few deviations made necessary by the topography of the peninsula. Flashy neo-Renaissance palaces and narrow, unconventionally decorated terrace houses with bay windows shot up out of the uneven ground.

Then, at daybreak on April 18th 1906, there was an earthquake the like of which nobody had ever experienced before. It lasted only a few seconds, but the earth was torn apart, pavements caved in and houses collapsed. Six hundred people were crushed or suffocated to death. Fire broke out, but could not be extinguished because the 'quake had ruptured the water pipes. So for a week the fire gradually, almost at its leisure, consumed the city. Twelve blocks between Polk Street and Van Ness Avenue had been spared by the 'quake, but they now had to be blown up in order to halt the fire.

Reconstruction began immediately, and proceeded with incredible energy and success. The earthquake was caused by a jolt in the San Andreas Fault, which runs diagonally through San Francisco. The danger, of course, remains – as was proved in 1989.

✕ Eating and drinking

San Francisco is a fine city for food-lovers. And America's best wines are produced close to San Francisco, in the Napa Valley.

The numerous restaurants and eating places often specialise in foreign cuisines: Chinese, Italian, German, Japanese, French. The following places are of proven quality and can be recommended. (In more expensive restaurants it is advisable to reserve a table.)

Alioto's (8 Fisherman's Wharf, 10.30 am–11 pm): a picturesque location on the wharf; has specialised in fish dishes since 1925. Fine view of the whole Bay.

Hong Kong (835 Pacific Ave, 8 am to late evening): Chinese tea-house; the dishes are brought to the tables on trolleys.

Caravansery (310 Sutter St, closed Sun.): Middle Eastern food, nice atmosphere.

Ciao (230 Jackson St): Italian, fashionable, fresh pasta and fish daily.

Fairmont Hotel, top floor (on Nob Hill, 11.30 am–2 pm, Mon.–Sat 6–10 pm): fantastic view over San Francisco. Not exactly cheap, but you can just have a cocktail, or brunch on Sundays.

House of Nanking (919 Kearny St).

House of Prime Rib (1906 Van Ness Ave, 5–11 pm): for lovers of large to enormous portions of meat. 'Prime rib' is a typical American beef speciality.

Jack's (615 Sacramento St): French, famous for more than 100 years.

Masa's (648 Bush St, open Tues.–Sat.): French cuisine, elegant, expensive.

Original Joe's (144 Taylor St, 10.30 am–1.30 pm): serves the largest and best-value hamburgers in San Francisco.

Post Street Bar and Café (632 Post St): a typical Californian restaurant.

Sam's Grill (374 Bush St, closed Sat. and Sun.): fresh seafood daily, moderately expensive, bursting at the seams

between 11.30 am and 2 pm. Eat before or after these times.

Schroeder's Café (240 Front St, closed Sat. and Sun.): an old-fashioned German utopia, adapted to American tastes. Sauerbraten, of course, and everything Americans desire in the way of German delicacies. Portions for lumberjacks!

Sear's Fine Foods (439 Powell St, 8 am–2 pm, closed Mon. and Tues.): ample breakfasts, American style.

Swan Oyster Depot (1517 Polk St, 8 am to late evening): a must for lovers of fish and seafood, serves a great clam chowder. Fresh oysters. Old-fashioned, but fashionable.

Tadich Grill (240 California St, 11.30 am–8.30 pm): founded in 1849, described by locals as *the* typical San Francisco restaurant.

Ten-ichi (2227 Fillmore St): very good Japanese restaurant; reasonable prices.

Tommy's Joynt: (corner of Van Ness Ave and Geary St, 10.30 am–11 pm): dozens of different beers from all over the world and home-made food at the buffet. Pub atmosphere and reasonable prices.

Vanessi's (498 Broadway, to 1.30 am, 12.30 am Sun.): outstanding Italian cooking, famous for its salads. Artists and business people among the clientele. The cook works in the middle of the dining room.

Yamato Restaurant (717 California St, 11.45 am–2 pm and 5–10 pm, closed Mon.): excellent Japanese food, tasteful décor.

ℹ️ Telephone numbers, for all eventualities: emergency 911; police 553 0123; emergency medical service (*San Francisco Medical Society*) 567 6230; emergency dental service (*San Francisco Dental Society Referral Service*) 421 1435; ambulance 931 3900; Traveller's Aid Society 781 6738.

Golden Gate Bridge, the Bay and the city beyond

Ex Around the Bay

The easiest way of travelling around the Bay is of course by car, but the most important and interesting places can be reached by bus or ferry. (Timetables from *Convention and Visitors Bureau*, see page 26.) Sausalito has its own ferry service.

By car: over the spectacular *Golden Gate Bridge* (US Highway 101) to the north bank of the Golden Gate. There are splendid views from the car-park after the exit from the bridge, as well as from the raised viewing-point on the opposite side of the road – the best view of the bridge and the city. A few miles further on, exit to:

Sausalito (pop. 7,500)

This lies directly on the Bay, at the point where it narrows into Richardson Bay; an attractive location for sailors, painters and tourists, with galleries, restaurants with fine views, a marina and a large hydraulically operated model of San Francisco Bay (*Delta Hydraulic Model*, 2100 Bridgeway).

Sausalito is in *Marin County*; the main attraction here is the *Muir Woods National Monument*, a nature conservancy area covering 0.8 sq miles (223 ha), with an extensive network of trails and imposing groves of redwoods (*Sequoia sempervirens*), some nearly 230 ft (70 m) high and more than 2,000 years old. The banks of fog rolling in from the Pacific and the stable climate of the north Californian coast provide ideal conditions for the redwoods. They grow in a coastal zone that is about 500 miles (800 km) long but only a little over 30 miles (50 km) wide. The roots of these giants only go down about 6 ft (2 m) into the ground, but extend over a radius of more than 45 yards (40 m)! Muir Woods is reached via US 101 and State Highway 1, 17 miles (27 km) north of San Francisco. (The strict rules of the American national and state parks apply here: no camping, no picnicking except in the specially designated area, no picking of flowers, berries or mushrooms. A trail map is available free of charge. Open daily until sunset.

In the vicinity are *Stinson Beach*, one of the largest bathing beaches in California, and the ornithologist's paradise

Sausalito

of *Bolinas* and *Point Reyes Beach*, where bathing is forbidden because of surf and currents, although walks along the coast are to be recommended: there are more than 50 miles (80 km) of footpaths. Seals can be seen here, and during the migration season (Dec.–Jan., Mar.–Apr.) whales may be spotted. There is a lighthouse, and a bit of history: Sir Francis Drake once landed here, although he left no traces of his visit. Return to US 101 and continue to:

San Rafael (pop. 45,500)
Founded in 1817 as the twentieth and most northerly of the Spanish missions in California, the dilapidated mission was faithfully restored in 1949. The pride of the town is the unusually designed *Civic Center*, the last great work of the architect Frank Lloyd Wright. It resembles a multi-storeyed bridge, which connects two hills and then continues to a third level. Even today the building has a futuristic air to it; it houses the city administration, the courthouse and the library.

Follow the signs to the *Richmond–San Rafael Bridge* (toll) and drive straight past *Richmond* and *Albany* to:

Berkeley (pop. 107,000)
Places of interest include the *Municipal Rose Garden*, with more than 4,000 varieties of rose, the *Pacific Film Archive* (2621 Durant Ave) and the *Charles Lee Tilden Regional Park*. All three lie in the shadow of the *University of California*,

which has its largest campus here, with a total of 30,000 students. Berkeley is one of the most important universities in the USA, and certainly one of the most progressive. It is renowned not only as one of the centres of the radical student movement of the late 1960s, but also as a centre of scientific excellence, particularly in basic research in the natural sciences. (Guided tours of the campus from the *Student Union Building*, Telegraph Ave, tel. 642 5215.)

Oakland (pop. 365,000)

Lies opposite San Francisco on the Bay; its port rivals that of its more famous neighbour, and it is also an important industrial city and commercial centre. Oakland used to be unpopular because of its high crime rate but now enjoys higher regard, thanks largely to its favourable land and hotel prices – and because of the view of San Francisco. During the height of the tourist season, Oakland represents a worthwhile alternative destination. It is linked to San Francisco by the Bay Bridge and the underground trains of the BART system.

The main place of interest in Oakland's port district is *Jack London Square*, with the *First and Last Chance Saloon* (Webster St); it is a bar and museum, formerly a favourite watering-hole of the famous author. Jack London, born in San Francisco in 1876, spent his youth in Oakland, so his name is constantly cropping up here, for example in *Jack London Village*, a district in turn-of-the-century style, with shops and restaurants.

In the middle of Oakland is *Lake Merritt*, actually a salt-water basin. It covers an area of a quarter of a square mile (60 ha) and offers facilities for many kinds of watersports, as well as a varied amusement park, with a fairy-tale garden, a

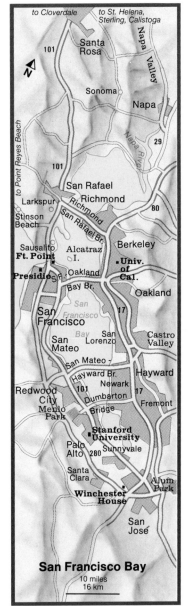

San Francisco Bay

10 miles
16 km

Japanese garden and cactus planta-
tions. The *Oakland Museum* (Tenth and
Oak Sts) houses temporary exhibitions
and an interesting permanent exhibition
on the ground floor on the theme of
'California'. Oakland also offers the *Kaiser Center* (a skyscraper which is the
headquarters of the Kaiser Group), a
Mormon temple (of which only the garden can be visited), the *Zoo* in Knowland
Park and the *Paramount Theater of the
Arts* (1931), a picture-palace from the
golden age of Hollywood which now
serves as an art gallery and concert hall
and which has achieved the status of
'historic place' (2025 Broadway). Finally,
the *Mission San Luis Rey de Francia*
(4050 Mission Ave, on Hwy 76, 4½
miles/7km) is a fine example of the old
Spanish mission stations in California.

From Oakland, you can either drive
over the Bay Bridge straight back to San
Francisco, or you can take the longer
route over the *San Mateo Bridge* from
Hayward to *San Mateo* (bridge toll) or
the even longer drive via Newark and
the *Dumbarton Bridge* to:

Palo Alto (pop. 56,500)

Seat of one of the most highly regarded
universities in America, *Stanford*, which
can be visited daily at 11 am and 2.15
pm. It was founded in 1885 as an ins-
titution for poor boys by the railroad
king Leland Stanford, in memory of his
only son. If you would like to visit the
world-famous *Stanford Linear Acceler-
ator Center*, the 'largest scientific instrument in the world', you should make
an appointment in advance (tel. 415
854 3300).

The many towns in the *Bay Area* –
San Lorenzo, Castro Valley, Fremont,
Santa Clara, Sunnyvale, Menlo Park,
Redwood City – have gradually merged
to form one of the most densely pop-
ulated conurbations in America, a world

centre of the microelectronics industry
and semiconductor production. San
José is also part of Silicon Valley.

San José

South-east of the Bay in Santa Clara
County, with 204,000 inhabitants in
1960. Twenty years later the figure was
600,000! The 'Garden City' owes this
phenomenal growth in part to the fertility of its fruit and vegetable farms, but
above all to the astonishingly rapid
development of its electronics and
transport industries. Founded in 1777
as *Pueblo de San José de Guadalupe*,
the village developed to become California's leading city. Its rapid growth was
triggered not by gold but by the mercury
ore that was mined in the vicinity. For
two years San José was the capital of
the brand-new state of California.

Places of interest: *Frontier Village
Amusement Park*, a funfair in the style of
the 1890s, the *Egyptian Museum*, *Alum
Rock Park*, with mineral springs, picnic
places and strange rock formations.

A special tip

The most original attraction in the
city is *Winchester House* (at the
intersection of I-280 and Hwy 17), a
bizarre monstrosity. Mrs Sarah Winchester, a member of the arms man-
ufacturing family, was obsessed by
the odd notion that she would live
for as long as building work continued on her house. So she continued
to have it extended. In the end, even
she needed a map to find her way
around the labyrinth of 160 rooms,
2,000 doors, 13 bathrooms, 40
staircases, many secret passages,
10,000 windows, trapdoors, and
narrow flights of stairs leading nowhere. The empty ghost castle is
open to visitors.

Ex Napa, the valley of wine

The Napa Valley, America's most famous wine-producing area, is a good hour's drive north-east of San Francisco. The valley runs in a shallow arc north-west from Napa town. Do not expect to find any scenic villages, half-timbered houses or châteaux. Even the landscape is hardly spectacular – though in autumn, when the Napa Valley is bathed in the loveliest colours, many visitors are attracted to the vineyards. The residents are of course proud that America produces not only cola and root beer but also wines of a quality that has truly alarmed the arrogant Europeans, with their 2,000-year tradition of wine-making. It is true that there are several places in the Napa Valley where the romantic vision of European wine-making is imitated – *Christian Brothers'* winery in *St Helena* (tel. 963 2719) looks like a 19th c. German station, built of solid stone with period decorations. There are free wine-tastings and guided tours through the wineries, as well as large crowds. But if you want to see how modern managers turn wine into an industrial product, visit the *Sterling Winery* (tel. 942 5151), between *St Helena* and *Calistoga*. The building can be seen from a long way off: it is snow-white and perched on a hill. Beaming girls in scanty uniforms greet you, and then a canary-coloured cable car whisks you up to the vineyards. Down below is a park, with lawns that have apparently been manicured with nail scissors. There is not a human being to be seen. This could be an espionage centre, or a psychiatric clinic for millionaires. You walk up open staircases and over clinically spotless roof

Christian Brothers' winery

terraces; the white walls interconnect and bells in the tower strike each quarter of an hour. You are directed into the air-conditioned citadel. Gleaming silver cylinders – a launching pad for intercontinental rockets? No, they are fermenting-vats. The place smells of nothing at all. There is a humming noise. Still no people. Written signs instruct you to follow the arrows, and inform you that eight different wines are produced here: Blanc de Sauvignon, Pinot Chardonnay, Gewürztraminer, Pinot Noir, among others. You walk and walk through the whole place, always screened off by glass, always accompanied by information charts and written signs. You always know what is happening behind the glass: here sugar is being broken down into alcohol and carbon dioxide, there the wine is resting and maturing. Eventually you find yourself standing in the open air. A pleasantly green valley, hills, fields where slowly crawling machines are at work. A shady terrace, and more smiling blondes. The wine may be tasted, provided you pay for it. You may sit down. The view is pleasing, the wine very cool, and there is a strong aroma of carnations. How about a bite to eat? Sorry, no. There is only wine here, and order forms. Nothing is at bargain price, however. The quality is very high: the Cabernet Sauvignon could be served in any restaurant in the world.

When the wine is sold, the label indicates not its origin but the grape variety from which it is made. The richly coloured *Cabernet Sauvignon*, with its full bouquet, and the *white Cabernet*, with its strong grape aroma, are probably the finest varieties. *Zinfandel* has long been considered the native Californian grape. The Napa Valley has an ideal but very complicated climate. Late frosts are rare, but not unknown.

Because of the unpredictable weather, the vintages are by no means as consistent as in the more southerly *Central Valley*, which does not, however, reach the same heights of quality as the Napa Valley.

The wineries are all along Hwy 29, beginning immediately beyond Napa and continuing up the valley as far as *Calistoga*: Christian Brothers, Robert Mondavi, Chappellet, Buehler, Louis Martini, Beringer, Inglenook, Charles Krug, Stony Hill and Schramsberg (sparkling wine) are some of the more famous. Not all offer wine-tastings, but many have gift shops selling all sorts of knick-knacks: glasses, corkscrews, coasters, wine baskets and pottery. If you want to sample the local wine on the spot, and need some French bread, ham and French cheese to go with it, you should stop immediately after the friendly little town of *Napa* at the *Vintage 1870* shopping centre, an excellent place to shop for your picnic.

The *Sonoma Valley*, a wine-producing area almost three times bigger than the Napa Valley, runs virtually parallel to the Napa, starting at Sonoma and extending northwards through *Santa Rosa*, along the *Russian River* to *Cloverdale*. The climate here is a trifle less certain even than in the Napa Valley, since the ocean and its fogs are closer.

Korbel (tel. 887 2294) make an excellent dry sparkling wine, which US legislation allows to be marketed as champagne. The *Italian Swiss Colony* (tel. 433 2333) at *Asti* produces respectable table wines in large quantities. *Dry Creek Vineyard* (tel. 433 1000) produces a dry *Chenin blanc* and has benches and tables outside for picnickers. (US 101 runs straight through the Sonoma vine-growing region.) A detour to the still waters of Clear Lake can be recommended.

The green north of California

Northern California is a land of giant redwoods, surf, fog, vast open spaces, mountains and lakes: an ideal holiday area for those who dislike museums. There are few towns, and no cities. The nightlife is limited to peaceful bars with juke-boxes. There is no nonsense about the food – steaks and fresh fish are the main attractions. You are always surrounded by forest. It rains a lot. American travel books on the Golden State tend to dismiss the north in a few lines.

Nevertheless, more and more people who have had enough of the cities in the south come up here to live. It is an area for nature-lovers, lumberjacks, loners, anglers and hunters (and for rattlesnakes). From June to September is the season for salmon-fishing, in August the Lumberjacks' Olympiad takes place and in October a marathon race is held through the redwoods. In spring and autumn grey whales can be seen as they migrate along the coast.

Giant redwoods, northern California

North of San Francisco, the Spanish place-names soon disappear; the Spaniards were not attracted by the rain-drenched primeval forests and the rocky, virtually inaccessible coast. The short rivers that wind their way down from the *Coast Range* to the Pacific are called the *Eel, Elk* and *Mad Rivers*. They are unpredictable in temperament: they tumble cheerfully through the valleys, and then suddenly rise up in spate, tearing away everything that gets in their way. Northern California's great natural resource is timber, particularly that of the redwoods, which is much sought after for house-building and commands a high price. It is pest-resistant and virtually fireproof. The people of *Fort Bragg* and *Eureka*, the only sizeable communities on the north coast, make their living from it.

There are three roads leading to the north. Hwy 1 hugs the coast, twisting and turning through innumerable bends: it's hard work, but incomparable, indeed essential if you want to marvel at the constantly changing views between the mountains and the Pacific. US 101 runs almost parallel to Hwy 1, but is less arduous; it affords no views of the sea until Eureka, however, although there are plenty of splendid panoramas on the long haul along the *Coast Range*. And finally, *Interstate Highway 5* leads from Sacramento to Red Bluff and through the *Shasta National Forest* to Oregon; this is the quickest route, and is one of the highways where the 65 mph speed limit applies.

Point Reyes, with the *National Seashore* of the same name, is a true paradise for hikers. It is also a breeding ground for the more than 300 species of birds that wheel and screech overhead, and home to more than seventy other species of animal. The place is linked to the open sea by a narrow, almost canal-like bay. Its harmless-sounding name, *Tomales Bay*, conceals its character as a geological villain of the first rank: it is the point at which the San Andreas Fault leaves the Californian mainland and dives beneath the Pacific. This fault is the line along which two major plates of the earth's crust meet, and it is never entirely peaceful.

Mendocino is a tiny place, an artists' colony with galleries, and the point of departure for the national forest of the same name. Very popular with hang-gliders, riders and hikers.

Fort Bragg (pop. 5,400)

A lumber town and the starting point for a rare pleasure: each day, the *California Western Railroad* runs a train from·here up to *Willits*, about 40 miles (64 km) inland. The return train journey lasts 7½ hours; fares are very moderate. The train is called the *Skunk* when it is pulled by a diesel locomotive through the wild valley of the *Noyo River*, over numerous bridges and through almost virgin forest. In summer the *Super-Skunk* runs – this is a steam locomotive straight out of the Wild West. (Information: California Western Railroad, PO Box 907, Fort Bragg, Calif., tel. 707 964 6371.) There are also shorter excursions from Fort Bragg or Willits.

Humboldt Redwood State Park

is a holiday area in the middle of protected redwood forests, with campsites but very few motel beds. The road running parallel to US 101 through the heart of the park is known as the 'Avenue of the Giants' – another reference, of course, to the giant redwood trees. This road, from *Phillipsville* to *Pepperwood*, crosses the *Eel River* at several points; the river offers trout-fishing

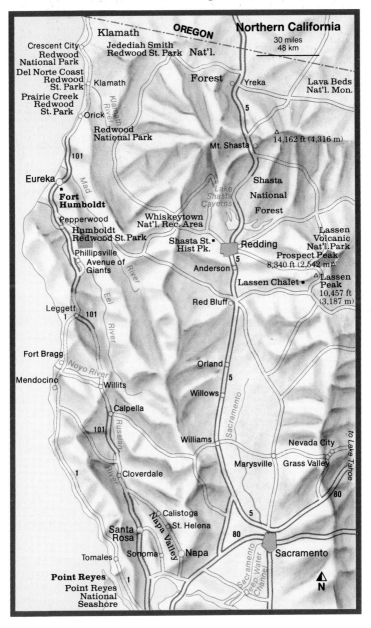

Klamath OREGON Northern California

Crescent City
Redwood
National Park

Jedediah Smith
Redwood St. Park Nat'l.

30 miles
48 km

Del Norte Coast
Redwood
St. Park

Klamath Forest Yreka

Lava Beds
Nat'l. Mon.

Prairie Creek
Redwood
St. Park

Orick

Klamath River

Redwood
National Park

Mt. Shasta

△
14,162 ft (4,316 m)

Eureka

101

Mad River

Shasta

National

Lake
Shasta
Caverns

Forest

Fort
Humboldt

Pepperwood

Whiskeytown
Nat'l. Rec. Area

Lassen
Volcanic
Nat'l. Park

Humboldt
Redwood St. Park

Shasta St.
Hist Pk.

Redding

Prospect Peak
8,340 ft (2,542 m)

△

Phillipsville

Avenue of
Giants

Eel River

Anderson

5

Lassen Chalet ■

△Lassen
Peak
10,457 ft
(3,187 m)

Leggett

1 101

Red Bluff

Fort Bragg

Noyo River

Orland

5

Sacramento

Mendocino

Willits

Willows

Calpella

101

Russian River

Williams

Nevada City

to Lake Tahoe

1

Cloverdale

Marysville

Grass Valley

80

Calistoga

Napa Valley

St. Helena

5

80

Santa
Rosa

Sonoma

Napa

Sacramento

Tomales

Point Reyes

Point Reyes
National
Seashore

1

Sacramento
Deep Water
Channel

N

In Redwood National Park

between May and November, while the season for salmon trout runs from November to January. Further information can be obtained from *The Avenue of the Giants Association* (PO Box 1000, Miranda, Calif.).

Eureka (pop. 25,000)

The largest town on the northern Californian coast. Its history and development have been fashioned by the ocean and the rich local timber resources. Redwood and Douglas fir are used in building, while a large fishing fleet constitutes the second element of the town's economy. At first sight Eureka is dominated by factories and warehouses. It also has a district of Late Victorian wooden houses, as well as *Fort Humboldt*, which was built in 1851 as a defence against Indians, and the *Clarke Memorial Museum*, containing weapons from that time.

Redwood National Park: a relatively narrow strip of magnificent forest scenery, wild coast, bathing places, azaleas in a range of vivid colours, white water and of course redwoods. US 101 reaches the National Park at *Orick* and leaves it again shortly before *Crescent City*. Somewhat confusingly, the *Del Norte*, *Jedediah Smith* and *Prairie Creek Redwood State Parks* also lie within the National Park.

Wild rhododendrons bloom in June. There are eighteen separate redwood groves, romantic bathing beaches, an *Indian Museum* and redwood carvings. The water is cold and treacherous, with unpredictable currents.

On the edge of the park is *Klamath*, on the *Klamath River*. River excursions on a roaring jetfoil leave Klamath at 9 am, returning about 3 pm. In summer, salmon swim up the river, attracting large numbers of anglers in pursuit of the 'king'. The *Klamath National Forest* is a nature conservancy area: there is no access for motor vehicles, although there are extensive trails for hikers. (Information: *Redwood National Park, Park Headquarters,* 1111 Second St, Crescent City, CA 95531, tel. 707 464 6101; *Redwood Information Center,* Orick, CA 95555, tel. 707 488 3461.)

A special tip

The *Lava Beds National Monument*, to the east of *Yreka*, can be reached by making a detour of some 60 miles (96 km). This may well be what the entrance to hell is like: gates of petrified lava, bizarre cinder cones, ghostly caves with ice more than a thousand years old and a horrific maze of crevices and tunnels. Any terror inspired by these pranks of nature is overshadowed by history: in 1872–3, eighty warriors of the Modoc tribe, led by their deputy chieftain 'Captain Jack', took shelter in the natural lava fortifications. The American government wanted to negotiate with the Modocs, and sent General Canby as their representative. The deputy chieftain had him captured and killed. Soon afterwards the army stormed the lava citadel; 'Captain Jack' was hanged.

Mount Shasta (pop. 3,500)

is named after the volcano *Mount Shasta*, 14,162 ft (4,316 m) high. It is no longer active. The neighbouring *State Fish Hatchery* raises a few doubts about the opulent, seemingly inexhaustible natural life in the area: each year, up to ten million trout fry supplied by this fish-breeding establishment are released into the waters of northern California. The name Shasta crops up again in the gigantic *Shasta National Forest* and the *Whiskeytown-Trinity-Shasta National Recreational Area*, north of Redding.

Redding (pop. 53,000)

The town has many hotels and is the departure point for excursions to the surrounding parks. Its turbulent history during the Gold Rush is preserved in the *Shasta State Historic Park*, 6¼ miles (10 km) to the west. Here there are buildings from the Wild West period, including the elegant residence of the surgeon Dr Shurtleff, who specialised in the removal of pistol bullets. The *museum* in Redding houses displays of Indian art and implements from the period before Columbus.

The *Lake Shasta Caverns* are caves that have been opened up for tourists; there are sightseeing tours by boat. The construction of the *Shasta Dam* created *Shasta Lake*, a much frequented paradise for watersports enthusiasts. Houseboats can be rented. (Information at the Visitors Center.) The Shasta Dam is the second highest in the world and can be visited, as can the associated power station. Admission free.

Winter sports areas

Northern California is not particularly well endowed with winter sports resorts, mainly because of its distance from the large centres of population. *Mount Shasta* is one of the best-known exceptions, and so is the *Lassen Volcanic National Park* at the southern end of the

Mount Shasta

Lassen Volcanic National Park

Cascade Range. The highest point is the imposing *Lassen Peak* (10,457 ft/ 3,187 m), a volcano that was last active in 1915, which made it America's most recently active volcano until a massive explosion blew the peak off Mount St Helens in 1980.

Lassen Peak, Prospect Peak (8,340 ft/2,542 m) and *Mount Harkness* (8,045 ft/2,452 m) are accessible by safe footpaths. A trip through Lassen Park will reveal that the earth underneath is still bubbling away – scalding hot springs spurt forth, hot mud gurgles, ponds and lakes steam, the underworld emits sulphurous fumes, the ground hisses and simmers. *Lassen Chalet* is a winter sports centre, although its facilities cannot compare with those in the Alps. (Information: *Lassen Volcanic National Park*, Mineral, CA 96063, tel. 916 595 4444.)

Sacramento (pop. 327,000)

The state capital of California since 1854. The city is rebuilding its past in *Old Sacramento*, with timber houses, wooden sidewalks, old-fashioned, hand-written menus and in the bank window a sparkling pair of scales for weighing gold nuggets; it would hardly surprise you to see John Wayne walking round the corner.

In the distance glistens the golden dome of the Californian *State Capitol*. Foreign visitors who have never visited an American State Capitol should take this opportunity to do so. Almost all of them are modelled on the 'mother house' in Washington DC, and Sacra-

State Capitol, Sacramento

Old Sacramento

mento is no exception: American Renaissance, with a flight of steps at the front, columns, statues of celebrities virtually unknown to European visitors, frescos and a lavish display of symbolism. The Californian State Capitol, restored in 1982, houses the state parliament (forty state senators and eighty assemblymen). The Californian constitution requires each voter to be able to read the constitution and write his or her own name.

Sacramento is a pretty place, with the grid-like street pattern that is usual in American cities, a lot of green spaces and its own modest art gallery (*Crocker Art Museum*, 216 O St), as well as a *State Indian Museum* (2618 K St) with a dug-out canoe, wickerwork and tomahawks. (Sacramento Convention and Visitors Bureau, 1100 14th St; Old Sacramento Visitor Center, 2nd/K Sts.) The harbour is the terminus for the *Sacramento River Deep Water Ship Channel*.

A special tip

Sutter's Fort (27th and L Sts) is a site of historic interest. Built in 1839 from air-dried bricks, it was the dramatic starting point in 1848 for the great Gold Rush, which transformed California at a stroke – and ruined 'General' John Sutter. The old buildings have been restored and augmented with period items. Visitors can listen on headphones to the exciting story of how the first gold was found on the bed of Sutter's millstream. And how Sutter lost all he had.

Wooden sidewalks, Old Sacramento

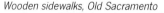

Through the Sierra Nevada

Distances are great and journey times long because of the strictly enforced speed limit. This section gives information on the most important places, some possible excursions and the national parks. It is best for individual travellers to decide for themselves – with the aid of a map, of course – which route to take, and whether to travel by hire-car or bus.

If you are coming from San Francisco and want to find your way into the Sierra via the holiday resorts around Lake Tahoe, it is best to take Interstate 80 from Oakland to Sacramento. At Truckee you will have to decide whether you want to go to the quieter west shore of Lake Tahoe, or to the east shore, with the obligatory sortie into the gambling state of Nevada. It takes about 4½ hours to drive from San Francisco to the lake.

An hour past Sacramento, the road begins to rise imperceptibly: the foothills of the Sierra are drawing closer. This was once Gold Rush country. California cares about its short, stormy past, and where buildings from the Gold Rush years have remained standing they have been skilfully nailed together and polished up. They are then often given the title of *historic park* – but don't let this deceive you into expecting something on the scale of Versailles or Windsor Castle.

Grass Valley (pop. 5,800)

This is the site of the *Empire Mine State Historic Park*, which was, for its time, a massive industrial complex, devoted to the extraction of gold ore. The Empire Mine is still operating and has nearly 200 miles (300 km) of galleries. In 1860 attempts were made to prospect for gold 'hydraulically'. Whole hillsides were washed away by water-jets.

A special tip

Lola Montez Cottage on Mill Street is a particular surprise. The Irish-born dancer, whose affair with King Ludwig I of Bavaria led to his abdication in 1848, kept a luxurious house here, with a bath, wine cellars and a menagerie. A bust of the King stood in a niche. Lola, dressed in bright red velvet and with an extremely daring décolletage, held court as 'the uncrowned queen of Grass Valley'.

Truckee

Nevada City (pop. 2,500)

Grass Valley's neighbour is not in Nevada at all, but still in California. There is another state park here, the *Malakoff Diggings State Park*, together with a museum and the *Old Nevada Theater*, built in 1865, the first theatre in California. At that time, the place was almost literally shooting up out of the ground: in the first year of the Gold Rush alone, 400 houses were built. Several of the old buildings are still standing, including *Fire House Number One* and the *National Hotel*.

Lake Tahoe (alt. 6,233 ft/1,898 m)

Encircled by mountains, the lake lies behind the main ridge of the *Sierra Nevada*. Its waters are clear, dark blue and ice-cold; during both the summer and winter seasons its shores are as overcrowded as the Lake District in a hot August. It is just over 20 miles (35 km) long and 12½ miles (20 km) wide, and only two-thirds of it is in California. The other third is in Nevada, where the laws controlling gambling are relaxed, to say the least. The splendid scenery and the Nevada nightlife account for the enormous popularity of Lake Tahoe.

South Lake Tahoe, with its many motels and small hotels, is in California. *Stateline*, however, is in Nevada. It is a town of luxury hotels, casinos and one-armed bandits. When you walk into a casino, it is as if you were entering a factory in which the same levers are always being pulled, the only interruption being the occasional clattering of a handful of coins rattling into the metal trays. The big hotels attract large audiences with shows by stars such as Frank Sinatra and Shirley MacLaine.

All sorts of accommodation are available around the lake, and there are also plenty of campsites. Boat trips depart from *Emeralds Bay* and from *Zephyr*

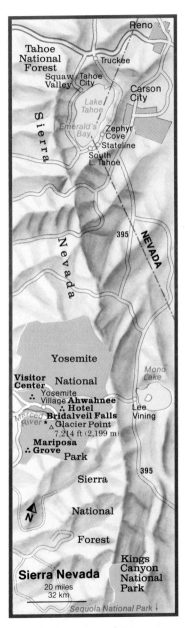

Lake Tahoe

Cove. The *Tahoe National Forest* is a good spot for bear-hunting and skiing.

From *Tahoe City* on the west bank of the lake it is not far to *Squaw Valley*, the site of the 1960 Winter Olympics. There are a further half dozen winter sports resorts scattered over the slopes of the Sierra on this side of the lake.

The Wedding Chapel in *Zephyr Cove* is highly recommended for couples wishing to get married. The brochure advertises: 'Intimate service by candle-light, taped organ music, altar decorated with flowers at no extra charge. Also special weddings in sailing boats, on horseback, in aeroplanes and on skis. Reasonable prices. We also accept credit cards'!

Ex *Reno* in Nevada (pop. 110,000) can easily be reached from Lake Tahoe in 30–60 minutes. The main industry of the 'biggest small town in the world' is tourism, encouraged by the casinos and the lavish stage shows. The one-armed bandits operate twenty-four hours a day.

On the northern edge of the lake are *Incline Village* and the *Ponderosa Ranch*, made famous by the long-running television series *Bonanza*. Many of the exterior shots were filmed in this area. The Ponderosa Ranch here is modelled exactly on the studio set and, to make it profitable, a whole Western town with souvenir shops has been built on the site.

The fastest route to the south and Yosemite is US 395, which follows the western slopes of the Sierra Nevada. On the way south, the landscape changes completely: the lush green of the mountain forests becomes paler and thinner, and the colour of the bare earth comes through, brown, greyish-brown and then finally grey. It is, in fact, one of California's many desert landscapes.

Mono Lake (alt. 6,402 ft/1,951 m) Situated high up in the mountains, glittering against an extensive backdrop of bare peaks, is Mono Lake, three million years old and now at risk of drying out because for the past forty years water has been abstracted from the lake to supply Los Angeles, more than 300 miles (500 km) away. The breeding grounds of hundreds of thousands of nesting birds are under threat, since the water level is sinking at a rate of 18 inches (45 cm) a year. Bizarre pinnacles

and platforms of tufa line the margins of the lake like grotesque abstract sculptures.

If you want to drive through the weird landscape around the lake, do not in any circumstances leave the metalled road surface: the sand is treacherous. Start from *Lee Vining* where, in the Information Center set up for the purpose, you will find plenty of information about the bitter struggle waged by environmentalists for the preservation of Mono Lake.

Yosemite National Park is always sure of inclusion in any list of the main sights of America. It is a region of magnificent mountain scenery in the Sierra Nevada, over 1,000 sq miles (3,072 sq km) in area and up to 10,900 ft (3,300 m) above sea-level, with waterfalls so mighty that they seem almost to be plunging straight from the sky, and sheer granite cliffs, ideal for rock-climbing.

Wedding chapel, Tahoe

Inspiration Point, Yosemite

Although Yosemite seems at first glance to be a relatively unspoilt area of forbidding natural beauty, closer acquaintance reveals the opposite. Nothing here is left to chance any more. It is a perfectly developed tourist area, with 250 miles (400 km) of roads, 750 miles (1,200 km) of footpaths, climbing-paths and hiking trails, its own newspaper, nine gift shops, teletext screens for deaf visitors and church services for Catholics, Lutherans, Baptists, Mormons, Jews and Seventh Day Adventists. There is a programme of 'prayer walks' and Christian sightseeing tours of the park. And a climbing school, excursions on horseback or hired bicycle, folk-dancing seminars, shuttle bus services, street theatre, courses in map-reading, mountain hikes to Mount Dana (13,041 ft/3,975 m high), and night-time trips by lantern-light to the Pioneer Cemetery.

There are more than half a dozen hotels, including the magnificent *Ahwahnee Hotel*, built in 1927. They are usually fully booked. And because many visitors, particularly young ones, arrive by train or bus, there is an efficiently organised shuttle service between *Merced* and the park.

The heart of the National Park, severely overcrowded at the height of the season, is *Yosemite Valley*, a glacier-carved canyon about 7 miles (10 km) long. Excellent roads lead through the valley on both sides of the *Merced River*. Soon after the entrance to the valley, the park authorities have chosen and signposted an *Inspiration Point*, which is intended to encourage visitors in their meditation. Next, on the right-hand side, come *Bridalveil Falls*, which thunder down from a height of 620 ft (189 m). And then, on the left, *El Capitan*, America's most famous rock-face, an almost vertical cliff of pure granite, rises to a height of nearly 3,600 ft above the valley floor – 7,569 ft (2,307 m) above sea-level. On this cliff, master mountain-climbers test their skills under extreme conditions. It is a mountain without romance; there is no yodelling, the climbers turn up in jeans, trainers and crash helmets, and alpine dairy farms are unknown. It is the most demanding obstacle course in the world, vertical and perilous.

Further into the valley, the Upper Yosemite Fall plunges more than 1,400 ft (436 m) down into the valley (provided there is sufficient water); together with the Middle and Lower Falls it forms *Yosemite Falls*, at 2,430 ft (741 m) the second highest in the world. In *Yosemite Village* there are hotels and other accommodation, a museum, films and information centres.

Glacier Point can be reached via a long detour. From a height of 7,214 ft (2,199 m), it offers a first-class bird's-eye view over Yosemite Valley and the Sierra.

Mariposa Grove (near the southern entrance to the park) and *Tuolumne Grove* (near the north-western entrance) are the two best-known sequoia groves (*Sequoia gigantea*).

If you are planning a long stay in Yosemite National Park, book your accommodation well in advance (Reservation Office, Yosemite Valley, Calif., tel. 209 372 4611) and obtain documentation and programmes of events from the Superintendent, PO Box 577, Yosemite National Park, CA 95389. You will be warned about bears and their insatiable appetite for chocolate, bread and jam, which should never, ever be left lying around your tent. The official recommendation to campers is: 'Hang your food on a tree, fifteen feet above the ground and ten feet from the trunk'!

The *Sierra Nevada* is a mountain range 500 miles (800 km) long, which rises virtually directly into the air, almost like a gigantic ship that has capsized in a flat landscape of desert, prairie and bush. Yosemite Valley and the other famous parks are only a small part of the long mountain range; even today, large parts of the Sierra are still almost inaccessible: a bleak, rugged territory, furrowed by canyons and torrential streams, with luxuriant vegetation in some areas, bare and lifeless in others, an impenetrable granite wall. The vast, motionless columns of the sequoias stand there, surrounded by endless forests of ordinary conifers, like venerable rulers and their humble followers – even though pines and firs in the Sierra can reach a height of about 165 ft (50 m).

Yosemite National Park

Sierra National Forest

The forest borders Yosemite to the south. It is a large vacation and hunting area, with trout streams, sequoias, hiking trails and simple accommodation for open-air holidays without big-city luxury.

Sequoia and Kings Canyon National Parks

Both parks offer outstanding natural beauty, and some impressive statistics: more than 2,000 varieties of plant grow here. Bears prowl through the extensive upland forests, the mountain lion, or puma, still lives here and the legendary golden eagle soars above the furrowed

Kings Canyon National Park

stems of the sequoias, which include some of the largest of their kind: *General Grant, General Lee* and *The Hart*, all over 260 ft (80 m) high. (*Grant Grove* is clearly signposted on Hwy 198 at Giant Forest.)

The best parts of both parks cannot be reached by either car or bus; to get there, you need a rucksack, time and the physical fitness to make your way along the excellently signposted trails. Or you can go on horseback, a very popular form of transport here over difficult terrain. Both parks, which are administered jointly, are a little less overcrowded and less intensively organised than Yosemite. (Information about events, the hiring of horses, and accommodation can be obtained from: *Hospitality Service*, Sequoia National Park, CA 93262, or the *Superintendent, Sequoia and Kings Canyon National Parks*, Three Rivers, CA 93271, tel. 209 565 3341.)

There is no road running from north to south through the parks. The *General's Highway* between *Grant Grove* and *Three Rivers*, which virtually links Hwy 180 and Hwy 198, leads in an irregular semicircle through the western part of the park and to some of its showpieces. The road is 45 miles (73 km) long and leads over *Big Baldy Saddle*, which is 7,644 ft (2,330 m) high. There is a modest road toll; it is worth paying, since the road will take you to several highlights, particularly *Giant Forest*, where there are large numbers of sequoias, including the *General Sherman Tree*, 275 ft (84 m) high and more than 3,500 years old.

Even if you are not planning long hikes through the Sierra (over the *High Sierra Trail*, for example, which from here leads east for about 75 miles (120 km) to *Mount Whitney*), *Giant Forest Village* is the starting point for several trails which will at least give you a taste of this mountain wilderness. You will need stout shoes. *Moro Rock*, 6,725 ft (2,050 m) high and safely accessible via steps, is a granite cliff rising above the canyons below. *Crystal Cave*, a stalactite cave with guided tours, can be reached by making a detour by car and then walking for half an hour. *Grant Grove* has an informative exhibition about the destructive exploitation of the sequoias in earlier times and the botanical and historical peculiarities of the giant trees. The *General Grant Tree*, 267 ft (81 m) high and 40 ft (12.3 m) in diameter at its base, has been growing here for about 3,000 years. The *General Lee Tree* and the *Hart Tree* are also famous specimens.

The only road that runs from east to west is Hwy 178, on the southern edge of the Sequoia National Park. It is a rewarding route, affording constantly changing views. Between *Bakersfield* and the foothills, it runs through dark green rows of orange-trees, which look as if they have been injected into the yellow desert soil. Almost immediately you are surrounded by steep granite cliffs. Waterfalls cascade, mountain streams rush noisily downhill and the mountain flanks change colour from sulphurous yellow to lilac. Suddenly, the canyon opens up and the panorama unfolds, while far below the *Kern River* sparkles. Old Shatterhand really ought to be waiting round the next bend.

Despite its beautiful name, *Lake Isabella* has a rather unkempt bathing beach. The road climbs up to *Walker Pass*. The mountains beyond are pure rock: raw material, without any green, brown or white trimmings. The Sierra Nevada seems less full of life, more primeval than European mountain ranges, because there are no embellishments here – no mountain villages, no church steeples, no alpine pastures,

huts, farms or wayside crucifixes. The desert lies constantly in wait, a void of sand, boulders and cliffs, in all the shades of a burnt-out clay oven – pink, whitish-grey, purple-brown. The leaves of the stunted plants are as sharp-edged as the blade of a lawn mower and as hard as dried-out shoe leather. The eastern edge of the Sierra is not suitable for human habitation, and the US Navy tests its weapons here.

Owens Lake is drawn on the map with dotted lines. It consists only of a shore – there is no water, at least not in high summer. For hundreds of miles the landscape is empty, filled only with knee-high scrub, the mountains seemingly cleared away. The only traces of human life are the concrete ribbon of US 395 and the electricity pylons.

Lone Pine (pop. 1,500)

This has one single sight, which can be seen if you look westwards from the main street: it is *Mount Whitney*, at 14,495 ft (4,418 m) the highest peak in the USA outside Alaska. The road from Lone Pine climbs to *Whitney Portal*, which lies at a height of 8,373 ft (2,552 m). From the large car-park a path leads to the top of the mountain, a distance of about 4½ miles (7 km). If you want to walk to the top – it is an easy climb – you will need a *wilderness permit* issued by the *Forest Ranger Station* in the town (tel. 714 876 5542). If there are already too many walkers on the way to the top, then you will not get a permit!

Lone Pine, a typical ribbon development with service stations, smart motels, a supermarket, bars, churches, eating houses and used-car sales, has been the setting for many westerns because of its photogenic surroundings. *Keeler*, about 12½ miles (20 km) away, is a ghost town, an abandoned settlement from the Gold Rush years.

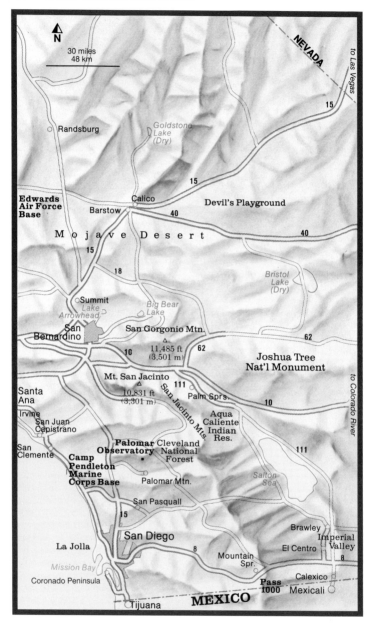

N

30 miles
48 km

to Las Vegas

NEVADA

15

○ Randsburg

Goldstone Lake (Dry)

15

Calico

Devil's Playground

Edwards Air Force Base

Barstow

40

40

M o j a v e   D e s e r t

15

Bristol Lake (Dry)

18

○ Summit

Lake Arrowhead

Big Bear Lake

62

San Bernardino

San Gorgonio Mtn.

△ 11,485 ft (3,501 m)

62

10

Joshua Tree Nat'l Monument

Mt. San Jacinto

△ 10,831 ft (3,301 m)

111

San Jacinto Mts.

Palm Sprs.

10

to Colorado River

Santa Ana

Irvine

San Juan Capistrano

San Clemente

Palomar Observatory ■

Cleveland National Forest

Aqua Caliente Indian Res.

Camp Pendleton Marine Corps Base

Palomar Mtn.

Salton Sea

111

San Pasquall

15

San Diego

La Jolla

Brawley

Mission Bay

8

Mountain Spr.

El Centro

Imperial Valley

8

Coronado Peninsula

Pass 1000

Calexico

○ Tijuana

MEXICO

Mexicali

Death Valley

Death Valley and other deserts

The most dangerous thing about Death Valley is its name. In this respect, it is in the same tradition as the geological phenomena with such expressive names as 'Coffin Peak', 'Dead Man's Pass', 'Grave Mountain', 'Dry Bone Gulch' and 'Dead Man's Golf Course'. You set off early in the morning. On the way you will see frequent warning notices with advice for drivers in the inferno of Death Valley. Over and over again you read: 'Caution! Because of the extreme heat, it is not recommended that you drive through Death Valley during the summer months, even if you are well prepared. However, if your journey is unavoidable, you should take supplies of water with you. Many travellers cross Death Valley at night when it is cooler.' At last you get into your car, breathing deeply. You have a feeling you might just be saying goodbye to life. The road is flat, grey and looks lifeless. You climb to 4,000 ft (1,220 m) and then drive on to *Townes Pass*, at a height of 4,954 ft (1,510 m). Absolute quiet. The road leads quickly downhill; you are plunging into Death Valley. You are now driving at sea-level. It is very hot. The road continues downhill. A bit of the desert here is called *Devil's Cornfield*. A lake shimmers in the distance, as unruffled as a mirror. Why isn't it shown on the map? Because it doesn't exist. It's a mirage: just hot, shimmering air. And the oasis out ahead there? The palm trees? The green? Is this all just an illusion too? No, the oasis is called *Furnace Creek*. It really exists.

It is very hot in summer: the highest temperature recorded (in the shade) is 56.6°C (133.9°F). In winter, Death Valley is a popular holiday area, with golf, tennis, riding and a reliable, dry climate. *Death Valley National Monument* covers an area of about 3,000 sq miles (8,000 sq km); it is not just a featureless desert, but a collection of all the possible desert landscapes. Undulating sand dunes cover the area between *Mosaic Canyon* and *Devil's Cornfield*; salt crystals glisten in the

Badwater

ghostly, graveyard quiet of *Badwater*; the staring eye of the *Ubehebe* crater gazes up at the merciless sun; the Sierra Nevada dozes on the horizon, veiled in a pinkish-blue haze; below *Zabriskie Point* the pressures in the earth's crust have squeezed the mountains together like the folds of a concertina; and the scorched slopes of *Manly Beacon* lie there like the earth's skeleton, gnawed away, lifeless, impassable. A real valley of death?

Nonsense. Death Valley is home to more than 500 varieties of plant and animal. And even the legend of how it got its name is not about corpses. In 1849, the year of gold fever, some travellers were trying a short cut to the Californian gold-fields and turned off the usual route. Their wheels became stuck. The animals perished; the heat was stifling; there was no water. They wandered on aimlessly. Because they could not agree on the route out, they divided into six groups — and finally escaped, by then reduced to emaciated, skeletal figures. From the top of *Panamint Range* in the west, one survivor turned to look down once more on the scene of their hellish ordeal and hissed: 'Goodbye, valley of death!' The series *Death Valley Days*, in which the young Ronald Reagan appeared, tells of the settlement of this area.

If you are interested in geology, in forms of life existing under extreme conditions, in the history of the American West and its adventurers, in one of the most extraordinary regions on the planet, then Death Valley will keep you busy for a week. If you have only a day — without an overnight stop — then *Furnace Creek*, with museums, plentiful information and maps, a hotel, restaurant and service station, can be recommended (Visitor Center and Monument Headquarters, tel. 786 2331). In one day it is perfectly feasible to visit *Devil's Golf Course* (grotesquely deformed salt deposits), *Badwater* (the lowest point in the continent, 282 ft (86 m) below sealevel — and very hot!), *Artists' Drive* (a one-way road through a wild, rocky region), *Golden Canyon* (for a strenuous but impressive short walk), *Zabriskie Point* (splendid panorama, very close to Route 190) and the sand dunes on the southern edge of *Mesquite Flat* (where the valley really does live up to expectations of what a desert should look like — although without camels).

Three sights in the *Death Valley National Monument* require longer detours:

Dante's View: a 26-mile (42-km) detour; the most impressive viewing point in the area, looking over the valley and Mount Whitney — the lowest and (outside Alaska) highest points in the USA.

Scotty's Castle: a fairy-tale castle in the far north of the valley, built in 1922 by an eccentric millionaire known as 'Death Valley Scotty'; open to visitors.

The *Ubehebe Crater*: also in the north, 56 miles (90 km) from Furnace Creek; the circular remnant of a volcanic eruption, 2,368 ft (722 m) in diameter and nearly 500 ft (150 m) deep.

In the absence of gold and silver, the prospectors shifted their attention to borax (disodium tetraborate, processed for use as a flux in welding and as a disinfectant). Parts of the old *Harmony Borax Works* (near Furnace Creek) have survived as a curious industrial ruin. You can find out everything you want to know about the borax trade in Death Valley in the Borax Museum in Furnace Creek.

The road network in Death Valley is first class. However, drivers are warned in the strongest possible terms not to depart from the metalled roads. Excursions on foot into canyons and abandoned mining tunnels can also be perilous. Apart from looking and taking photographs, almost everything is forbidden – picking flowers, collecting rocks or stones, feeding animals, camping overnight in the open air, gathering firewood.

All animals and plants are strictly protected. The horned lizards and snakes do not attack humans. The bighorn, a silver-grey cousin of the Alpine ibex, is seldom seen. More frequently spotted are groups of the 2,000 wild donkeys (*burros*), descendants of animals which escaped from the famous teams of twenty which were used to pull pioneer wagons. (Information: Death Valley National Monument, Death Valley, CA 92328.)

Scotty's Castle

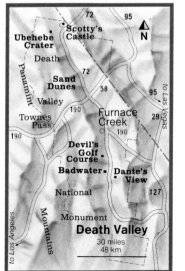

Calico ghost town

The Mojave Desert

In April 1981 the first American space shuttle, *Columbia*, landed on the concrete runway at *Edwards Air Force Base*, an hour-and-a-half's drive north of Los Angeles; the base is in the middle of the desert which makes up the largest part of south-eastern California: the *Mojave Desert*.

The name (pronounced Mo-há-vi) is an Indian word that was taken over by the Spanish. Its English name is the High Desert, because it lies at relatively high altitude, about 2,000 ft (600 m) above sea-level, rising to 6,500 ft (2,000 m). It is a hot region, a scorching oven, stretching from the mountains behind Los Angeles, over the ruler-straight border and into the state of Nevada – an area of around 15,000 sq miles (39,000 sq km). It was here that Walt Disney made his famous – and controversial – documentary *The Living Desert*. For, like most deserts, the Mojave is by no means a wasteland of pure sand, but a complex, many-sided ecological zone. The collared lizard suns itself on orange-red rocks, the Joshua tree's stumpy, contorted branches bloom at the end of March, rabbits and tortoises live in the scrub, and agaves raise their tall flower-stalks aloft; but only seldom will you hear the hissing, whirring warning signal of the only animal that bears the name of this desert: the Mojave rattlesnake. By day, desert animals hide in the shade; not until the searing heat subsides does the desert spring into life. The most widespread family of plants in the Mojave is the cactus, which is native to America and has developed hundreds of different species.

Unless you are directing a Western or taking part in a survival training course, the Mojave Desert is a region you will just pass through. There are no large towns. A look at the map will reveal the nature of this enormous sandpit: after the names of *Goldstone Lake, Emerson Lake, Bristol Lake* and two dozen other lakes the word 'dry' is printed in brackets. And the extensive area between Routes 15 and 40 is known aptly as the *Devil's Playground*.

The main town in the Mojave Desert is *Barstow* (pop. 20,000). The only place of interest is 10 miles (16 km) north-east, the ghost town of *Calico*. Between 1881 and 1896 silver worth $14 million (at historical prices) was mined here. Then the price of silver fell, and the town went bankrupt. South of Calico is the first solar-powered power station in the US, *Dagett*; it is open to visitors.

Other relics of the gold and silver boom include *Tropico Gold Mine* (south of the town of *Mojave*), where visitors can pay to poke around in gold-bearing rock debris and visit the inevitable museum, and *Randsburg* (north-east of Mojave), where you feel as if you are walking around in a picture-book of the old Wild West. Panning competitions are held for tourists.

Joshua Tree National Monument

In the south-east of the Mojave Desert, between Hwy 62 and Interstate 10, lies the Joshua Tree National Monument. It is a protected area, containing 780 square miles (2,000 sq km) of both the Mojave and Colorado Deserts. It owes its unusual name to the prickly *Joshua tree*, a strange tree which is in fact a species of yucca. Its branches look like those in children's drawings – they do not taper. At the end of the grotesquely distorted arms are clusters of sharp-edged leaves, as hard and as pointed as daggers. In addition to the Joshua trees, there are the usual set pieces of North and Central America's deserts: prickly-pear cacti, barrel and organ-pipe cacti, saguaros, agaves, moonflowers and the Spanish Dagger, a cousin of the Joshua tree. The region is hilly, rising to a height of over 5,500 ft (1,700 m) at *Keys View*, a splendid viewing point. (Information: Joshua Tree National Monument, 74485 National Monument Drive, Twentynine Palms, CA 92277.)

Salton Sea

South of the Joshua Tree National Monument is a geological curiosity: the Salton Sea, a salt-water lake 34 miles (55 km) long. It is almost as salty as the Pacific, which is nearly 100 miles (150 km) away; however, it has its origins in a catastrophe which happened in 1905, when the *Colorado River* burst its banks and flooded the trough scooped out in prehistoric times by the *Gulf of California*. This was a blessing for the tourist industry, for the Salton Sea is warm enough in winter for swimming, sailing and water-skiing. The lake is well stocked with fish, so that anglers can also enjoy this caprice of nature.

Imperial Valley

Imperial Valley, south-east of the Salton Sea, is another of California's 'natural wonders': it has the largest population in the world *below* sea-level. The hot, humid climate makes possible several harvests per year; tomatoes and strawberries ripen in December. This agricultural paradise is irrigated with water from the Colorado River.

El Centro (pop. 25,000) is 55 ft (17 m) below sea-level and is the largest town in Imperial Valley. In neighbouring *Brawley* the *Imperial Valley Rodeo*, a daredevil entertainment for tough types, is held each November.

Calexico–Mexicali

The twin cities of Calexico and Mexicali straddle the border between the USA and Mexico. *Calexico* is on the Californian side; *Mexicali*, which is ten times larger, is on the Mexican (and much more interesting) side. Foreigners can easily cross the border: only a passport is required.

Interstate 8, which crosses over from Arizona and continues to San Diego, is said to be the most scenically beautiful highway in the west. It runs between *Mountain Springs Pass* (about 3,280 ft/1,000 m high) and the Pacific, through the canyons and picturesque mountains of old Indian country.

Palm Springs

Palm Springs (pop. 33,000)

The centre of attraction in the southern California hinterland between sea and desert is Palm Springs, one of the few famous spas in America. It is an elegant health resort, an oasis in the Colorado Desert, and home to 1,000 millionaires. There are branches of expensive clothes shops and jewellers from Los Angeles, luxurious hotels and no fewer than thirty-seven golf courses, which is why Palm Springs likes to advertise itself as the 'golf capital of the world'. There are also 120 tennis courts.

The climate is warm and dry. As a result, the main season here is not summer (when the hotels offer generous discounts), but between December and March. Palm Springs is a very expensive spot, designed to meet the requirements of its wealthy clientele, stars from nearby Hollywood and major politicians; more than 100 film stars are said to have holiday homes there. In *Palm Canyon Drive* and the covered *Desert Inn Fashion Plaza* you can buy everything offered by smart shops in New York, Beverly Hills, Paris and Florence. Also of interest are the Desert Museum (101 Museum Drive) and the Moorten Botanical Garden (South Palm Canyon Drive).

The town owes its sheltered position to the *San Jacinto Mountains* (10,831 ft/ 3,301 m). The *Palm Springs Aerial Tramway* offers a quick route up the mountains: in fourteen minutes the cable car will take you 8,500 ft up. Another place of natural beauty worth visiting is *Palm Canyon*, which is about 6 miles (10 km) south of the town, on the Agua Caliente Indian Reservation. The canyon is an oasis of green, with over 3,000 palm trees, the oldest of which have already seen 2,000 summers. The bottom of the canyon can also be visited – on foot.

San Bernardino (pop. 140,000)

It owes its existence to Catholic missionaries and Mormon pioneers, and is noted for its orange-groves and vineyards. The prosperous agricultural and industrial town lies at the foot of the *San Bernardino National Forest*. Even the approach to the town is famous, the *Rim of the World Drive* (Hwy 18) to *Lake Arrowhead* and *Big Bear Lake*, a panoramic route that rises to over 6,500 ft (2,000 m). A great attraction for local children is *Santa's Village*, while the skiing area known as *Snow Summit* is popular with all ages. The highest peak in southern California, *San Gorgonio* (11,485 ft/3,501 m), is nearby; there are excellent campsites and splendid hiking trails through the mountains.

Ex Detour to Nevada

If your time in California allows, you should make at least one detour into the neighbouring state of Nevada, either from Death Valley or from anywhere in the Mojave Desert – to Las Vegas. Even if it turns your stomach, 'Vegas' really is worth seeing.

Las Vegas (pop. 165,000)

It is in the middle of the desert, but you wouldn't know it. Your line of vision is blocked by hotels, in which each year 11 million visitors take a breather from the tiring business of collecting – and losing – money. In 1931, the former silver-mining town was on its uppers. Then came salvation: the state of Nevada lifted the prohibition on gambling and suddenly casinos began to spring up out of the empty desert. Gambling (one-armed bandits, pontoon, poker, baccarat, blackjack and even bingo) is the only industry in Vegas. The large hotels have vast gaming halls, and almost every shop places one or two one-armed bandits at its customers' disposal. The large casinos advertise amazingly cheap meals and drinks, but of course there is a catch. People who have eaten cheaply and been plied with free drinks can easily be persuaded to try their hands at the gaming tables.

As early as breakfast-time the gaming halls are a hive of noisy activity, filled with the clatter and rattle of the chips. You can start cheaply, with five-cent coins, go on to quarters and end up on whole dollars. Millions of visitors spend their holidays in Vegas in this way, hard at work endlessly feeding the machine until it delivers, then raising the stakes, feeding the machine, losing, losing again, raising the stakes, raising the stakes again, fumbling for the free champagne – from seven o'clock in the morning until after midnight. The casinos never close. Luck lies in wait right round the clock. Of course there are suicides, but the local newspapers don't pay much attention to them. The biggest stars of international show business – Sinatra, Diana Ross, etc. – appear in Las Vegas in lavishly staged shows. Seats are relatively cheap, for even these spectacular occasions have only one purpose: to provide entertainment for casino customers and thus persuade people to come to Las Vegas.

The only sight of any interest in Las Vegas is *The Strip* (Las Vegas Boulevard), especially at night. In the middle is a wooden chapel – not for offering comfort to gamblers who have lost their last quarter, but for weddings! Yes, you can get married here – quickly, cheaply and without formalities. All cheques accepted, 24-hour service!

The sun shines 320 days a year. The heat is dry and bearable. Light clothing is recommended, with perhaps a small fur – not because of cool evenings in Vegas, but because of the icy blasts from the air conditioning in the casinos. And don't forget: on balance, the casinos always win...

Las Vegas

Horton Plaza shopping mall, San Diego

San Diego (pop. 1,000,000)

The second largest city in California has a mild, warm climate all the year round, extensive beaches, and wide green spaces on its undulating hillsides. There are lagoon-like bays, and splashes of decoration everywhere on the imitation Spanish-Mexican architecture. In the northern suburb of *La Jolla* San Diego is elegant, around *Mission Bay* it is obsessed with sport, and in *Balboa Park* cultivated and artistic. There is a long list of sights, although it includes nothing of the very first rank.

 ## History

For a New World city, San Diego has an unusually long history. The place was discovered in 1542 by the Portuguese round-the-world sailor Cabrillo, but more than 200 years passed before the Spanish priest Junipero Serra built a station above the natural harbour – the first of the twenty-one Californian missions. That was in 1769, and the mission was dedicated to San Diego de Alcalá.

Sightseeing

If you have the use of a car and a free day, the easiest thing is to follow the signs with a white seagull against a blue background. This *52 Miles Scenic Drive* will take you to virtually all the worthwhile viewing points, sights and interesting districts in the city. Even without your own vehicle you have plenty of scope; the bus systems are well integrated, bus routes extend everywhere within the main urban area, and fares are reasonable. (Up-to-date information on prices, events and exact opening hours can be obtained from *San Diego Convention and Visitors Bureau,* 1200 3rd Ave, tel. 232 3101, or in the larger hotels.)

The city has a complicated layout. On

the southern side a thick, pointed finger of land curves out into the ocean, creating a great bay with islands and peninsulas. On the northern side too the sea has found its way inland, this time leaving behind the islands and peninsulas of *Mission Bay*, with its labyrinth of channels for sailing boats and windsurfers.

The harbour

San Diego is above all a seaport, and a boat trip round the harbour is essential if you wish to get a feel for its individuality and importance (from Broadway and Harbor Drive; one-hour or two-hour trips). From the water you can see that the broad sweep of the city, silhouetted against the hills, is not dominated by any real skyscrapers. This is because the airport is in the middle of the city, and for safety reasons no building may exceed a height of thirty storeys. The city is sheltered from the open sea by the massive bulk of the *Coronado Peninsula*, the centrepiece of which is one of America's most elegant hotels, the sumptuous *Hotel del Coronado*, a Late Victorian summer residence for admirals, captains and millionaires. It was here that the future King Edward VIII is said to have met the American divorcée Wallis Simpson, a meeting that led eventually to the King's abdication. Today the peninsula and the beautiful Coronado Beach are dominated by a more modern sort of colossus: the aircraft carriers of the American Navy. One of the nuclear-powered giants, which carry nuclear arms, 100 aircraft and a crew of 5,000 men, is almost always berthed at the jetty. There are also cruisers, destroyers and submarines: in all, a third of the US Navy is based here. The harbour is also the home of the largest tuna-fishing fleet in the USA.

Another sight with maritime associations is the *Cabrillo National Monument* (at the very end of Catalina Boulevard). From December to February this is a prime spot for observing the annual southern migration of the grey whales. It is said, although it is difficult to believe, that the monument and the old lighthouse are America's most popular sights, attracting more visitors than even the Statue of Liberty in New York. At the end of the peninsula, *Point Loma Lighthouse* juts south into the Pacific; it is over 100 years old and is a splendid viewing point.

A special tip

The *Sea World Aquatic Museum* is in the resort area of *Mission Bay*, a maze of waterways and islands. For once superlatives are not out of place: it is the largest 'oceanarium' in the world, a maritime fairground spread over an area of more than 75 acres (30 ha), with sharks, dolphins, sea-lions, and *Shamu* the killer whale (entrance fee; open daily from 9 am to dusk). Mission Bay has several miles of beaches, and you can fish, picnic, go water-skiing or hire sailing boats.

Sea World, San Diego

Balboa Park

This extensive park offers a wide range of attractions, although this time without water, and even the large public golf course is not the centrepiece. Balboa's attractions are primarily cultural: it is a large square of peace and tranquillity in the middle of the city, dominated by a Spanish-style tower. There are palm trees and bougainvilleas, picnic tables and, in the Spreckels Pavilion, the largest organ in the world. The *Botanical Building* houses a good collection of tropical and subtropical plants, while the *Old Globe Theater*, which hosts a summer drama season, is a replica of Shakespeare's London theatre. The splendid *San Diego Museum of Modern Art* (Laurel St) has a first-class collection of European paintings, American naïve paintings, and contemporary sculpture. The *Science Center* (tel. 238 1168) houses some astonishing examples of modern museum technology; it is part of the *Reuben H. Fleet Space Theater and Science Center*, which also has a planetarium and a multi-media space show that simulates a flight into the galaxy.

And finally, Balboa Park is also the home of the famous *San Diego Zoo*, one of the largest zoos in the world, with 3,400 animals representing 750 different species. Cages are hardly visible — the animals live in surroundings that simulate their natural environments: jungle, desert, South Seas and mountains. The *Skyfari Tramway* offers an aerial perspective, and moving walkways facilitate the control and movement of visitors. Lions, elephants and giraffes walk around in virtual freedom, while the monorail carries you safely overhead. (The *San Diego Wild Animal Park* is about 28 miles (45 km) north of the city on US Interstate 15, near *San Pasqual*.)

Old Town San Diego State Historic Park

This is nothing like as pompous as the name suggests. It is not a real park either, but a reconstruction of old buildings in the Spanish-Mexican style. The site is genuine, for it was here, northwest of the present-day city centre, that the original village of San Diego sprang

Balboa Park, San Diego

up 200 years ago and the settlement of California by whites began. In the reconstructed 'Old Town' are shops, restaurants, the Serra Historical Museum, a library and the Tower Gallery.

Maritime Museum

The three-masted barque *Star of India*, built in 1863, is said to be the oldest floating iron ship. It is berthed at the Embarcadero (Harbor Drive and Ash St) and forms part of the Maritime Museum, as do two other windjammers, the *Medea* and the *Berkeley*.

The long sandy beach to the north of the city, stretching as far as Del Mar, offers plenty of opportunities for swimming. If you are interested in surfing, you can get all the information you need by phoning 714 225 9494. The waters around San Diego are dotted with sailing boats. Visitors can hire equipment or charter larger boats. (For information about this and many other things, including bicycle hire, golf courses, tennis facilities, fishing and riding, apply to the *Convention and Visitors Bureau*.)

Ex South of the border – *Olé!*

San Diego lies almost on the Mexican border, and nearly every visitor makes the trip across to *Tijuana*. The city has a reputation as a paradise for those bitten by either the shopping or the marriage bug. Express marriages (and divorces) are cheap. There is no difficulty about crossing the border, provided you show your passport and also fill in a *tourist card* if you intend to stay more than seventy-two hours in Mexico. If you intend to take your hire car with you, make sure your rental agreement includes insurance cover for Mexico. If it does not, you *must* obtain extra cover before you cross the border!

Downtown San Diego

Tijuana (pop. 850,000)

is in the Mexican state of *Baja California* (Lower California), the tongue of land that extends for almost 1,250 miles (2,000 km) between the Pacific and the Gulf of California. There are no great sights to see in Tijuana. Its irresistible charm lies in the fact that it is completely different from San Diego, its North American neighbour. When you cross the border, you will immediately feel that you have left one world and crossed into another – the quite different world of Latin America. Tijuana is an industrial city. The wide sidewalks are crowded and the shops are full of supposedly duty-free perfume, souvenirs, silver jewellery, leather jackets, spirits and all sorts of junk. There are exotic food shops, cheap restaurants, street cafés and bars and, on Sundays at 4 pm, bullfights, often featuring star toreadors from Spain (May to September; Arena Plaza Monumental and Arena El Toreo de Tijuana). There is another exotic sport: the fast-moving ball game *jai alai*, a version of the Basque *pelota*, which is played in the gracious *Frontón Palacio* (Avenida Revolución and Calle 7a).

Los Angeles
(pop. 3.1 million; pop. of urban area 11 million)

The actual municipality of this name merges imperceptibly with Long Beach, Glendale, Whittier, Beverly Hills, East Los Angeles, Downey, Santa Ana and San Fernando, to say nothing of Hollywood and Venice, Pasadena, Santa Monica, Huntington Park, Inglewood and Maywood, Alhambra, La Habra and Anaheim, to form the huge metropolis of Los Angeles, which covers an area of some 1,500 sq miles (4,000 sq km). It takes more than an hour to drive on one of the notorious freeways across Greater Los Angeles from San Fernando in the north-west to Santa Ana in the south-east, without stopping, without traffic jams, and sticking all the time to the maximum permitted speed.

Los Angeles cannot really be visited on foot. You can drive and drive on the more than 300 miles (500 km) of freeways, searching for the real heart of the city. But Los Angeles is no ordinary city. And it is only called Los Angeles on maps. Nobody who lives there says Los Angeles. They just say LA.

LA has almost become the largest city in the USA. It is certainly the place with the longest and most beautiful name: *El Pueblo de Nuestra Señora la Reina de los Angeles de Porciuncula*, in English 'The village of Our Lady Queen of the Angels in Porciuncula'. Its original wealth came from its cattle pastures. However, the Mexican mission did not exactly flourish, since the inhabitants were interested less in eternal life than in easy money, pleasure, throwing dice, playing cards and womanising. The *padres* made every effort, but to no avail. Despite the resonance of its pious name, Los Angeles is to this day a place for affairs of this world. (Many of its inhabitants consult psychiatrists for their spiritual needs!) Despite its many blemishes, LA is an irresistible magnet for tourists. Other flourishing industries include film, television and every other form of entertainment, electronics, air-craft construction, oil and the trans-shipment of goods.

Downtown Los Angeles is difficult to locate, but is usually taken to be the area around the *Civic Center*, a complex of functionally designed multi-storey buildings, including the *City Hall*, with its observation deck on the twenty-seventh floor, the *Music Center*, home of the splendid *LA Philharmonic Orchestra*, and several theatres. The cylindrical towers of the *Bonaventure Hotel* glisten in the sun, and from *Sunset Boulevard*, after dark, there is an extensive view over the glittering plain to the sea. For a few blocks along *Wilshire Boulevard* and *Hollywood Boulevard* the attractions of the big city make themselves evident. In *Beverly Hills* and *Pasadena* vegetation spreads extravagantly over fortress-like villas. But nowhere does the City of the Angels ever really acquire the exuberant atmosphere of big cities like New York and San Francisco. The old joke about 'fifty suburbs in search of a city' is not far wide of the mark.

Wild statistics, which nobody ever checks, are part of everyday life in LA. One of these can be verified, however: every day, five million cars move through the Greater Los Angeles area.

They would grind to a halt without the *freeways*, multi-lane highways driven mercilessly through the urban jungle; they repeatedly become entwined in fantastical, multi-level clusters, but they are the arteries along which the life-blood of the city flows. If you have arrived by car, you should make a point of memorising the main sections of the freeway system. At first sight they seem hopelessly entangled, with the access points often as well concealed as a state secret. However, they make it possible for visitors in a hurry to cover the far-flung sights of LA in a few days. The freeways are toll-free and there are plenty of exit points. A street map is essential if you are serious about trav-elling around LA. The most important routes into LA all connect directly with the freeway system.

Drivers should be aware that pedes-trians always have priority. Because LA is the most highly motorised metropolis in the world, the public transport system has been neglected. There are, how-ever, the buses of the *Southern Cali-fornia Rapid Transit District* and a *minibus system* which serves most of the business districts and the major hotels. But LA, unlike New York or San Francisco, does not have a well-

Los Angeles skyline

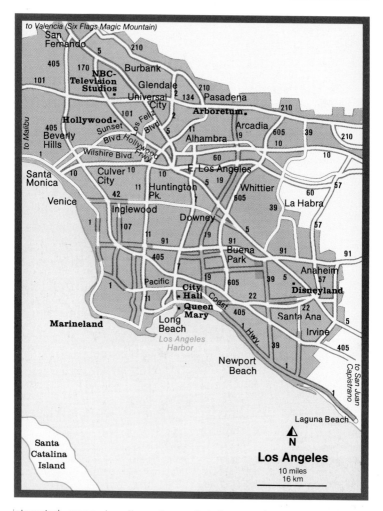

to Valencia (Six Flags Magic Mountain)

Los Angeles

10 miles
16 km

integrated mass transit system. Because of the long distances, taxi journeys are fairly expensive.

The climate is mild and reliable. It is often described as 'Mediterranean'. In the days when film material was not very sensitive and exterior shots could only be taken in bright sunshine, the film industry moved to nearby Hollywood because of the many sunny days it enjoyed. LA's climate would be virtually perfect if it were not for the notorious smog, an unhealthy mixture of natural humidity and exhaust fumes. The early morning news bulletins on radio and television issue warnings on days when

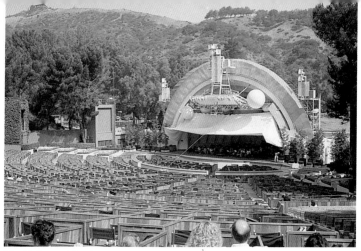

The Hollywood Bowl

the levels of air pollutants exceed the limit that can be tolerated by sensitive lungs. The smog has improved slightly since the city began to bury most of its waste material instead of burning it (a typically Californian solution). However, if the day is clear, you can observe from the twenty-seventh floor of the City Hall (North Spring St) how LA and its neighbours have filled the space between the *San Gabriel Mountains* and the Pacific with industry and concrete highways, sharp-edged skyscrapers and millions of houses, airports and harbours and fairgrounds, car-parks, oil derricks and church towers. Total urbanisation. An unimaginable, endless, motorised, air-conditioned plain, dotted with waving palm trees, irrigated by the distant Sierra Nevada, inhabited by people with white, black, brown and yellow skins, including film stars, psychiatrists, surfers, astrologers, millionaires, dolphins, body-builders, Mickey Mouse and Superman.

How to find your way about

Information about excursions, prices, events, opening times and bookings for shows in a television studio can be obtained at the *Greater Los Angeles Convention and Visitors Bureau* (Arco Plaza, 505 South Flower St, Level B, tel. 488 9100) in downtown LA. Hotels and motels distribute free calendars of events to their guests, particularly the useful *Where* magazine. The *Los Angeles Sunday Times* publishes an informative weekly list of events. *Key Magazine* also publishes up-to-date information. They all provide details of the elegant, luxurious and fashionable places where the wealthy of LA buy their clothes and jewellery and go to eat. And if you want to see what can only be seen here, then you can book a seat on the 'See the homes of the stars' excursion organised by the Star Line Company (tel. 463 3131; 6845 Hollywood Blvd). You will be driven in an air-conditioned limousine to the villas of famous film stars. And if you are interested in stars of the past, you can buy a guide to the graves of Hollywood stars like Clark Gable and Humphrey Bogart. On the other hand, if animals are more your line, you can see sea-lions and pelicans during a *Bay Cruise* (from Santa Monica Pier, Ocean Ave and Colorado, every hour; tel. 393 1993).

Disneyland

📷 Sightseeing

The sights in the Los Angeles area are so far apart that it is virtually impossible to plan a logical sequence of visits. The following selection is arranged alphabetically.

Arboretum (in Arcadia; 301 North Baldwin Ave). A research institute where trees and shrubs are cultivated. There are greenhouses full of orchids, and buildings constructed in various historical styles. Daily tours of the grounds.

Chinatown (North Broadway and Street of the Golden Palace). Restaurants, shops of all kinds, especially Oriental knick-knacks, jade, silk and lacquer-ware. Not as self-contained as Chinatown in San Francisco.

Civic Center (between Sunset Blvd, Grand Ave and First St). An area of administrative and cultural buildings, with green spaces and a certain degree of architectural charm. From *City Hall* (200 North Spring St) there is a fine panoramic view of LA and the surrounding area. The lift to the observation deck is free.

The *Music Center* (First St and Grand Ave) consists of three buildings for symphony concerts, drama and chamber music. The LA Philharmonic Orchestra is first class. Guided tours.

Disneyland (in Anaheim, 1313 Harbor Blvd, open until midnight in summer; tel. 714 999 4565 or 213 626 8605). Perfectly organised entertainment for children of all ages. The admission fee entitles you to partake of all the attractions, including *Space Mountain* (a roller-coaster with breathtaking descents; those suffering from heart trouble are warned!), *Jungle Cruise* (in boats through a cunning imitation of a primeval forest with amusing displays by wild animals – also artificial, of course), *Submarine Voyage* (with original optical and acoustic effects), and *Main Street, USA* (a nostalgic reproduction of a classic American small-town street, with town hall, ice-cream parlour, railroad station with steam locomotive, and parades featuring Mickey Mouse and all the characters made famous by Walt Disney). Other attractions include the Matterhorn Bobsleds, a modern ride which takes as its theme 'Children throughout the World', and journeys to Mars, up the Mississippi on a paddle-boat, through fairyland or the Wild West, into the future, to New Orleans and through a ghost castle. And then there are hamburgers, ketchup, popcorn, spaghetti, vanilla ice-cream, root beer, live music, souvenirs, a monorail and a cinema.

Farmers Market (Fairfax Ave and Third St) was once simply that, a market where farmers sold their produce. It has now gone up in the world, with smart shops and restaurants scattered among the fruit and vegetable stalls.

Forest Lawn Memorial Park (1712 South Glendale Ave) is America's famous cemetery. At first glance it looks like an extensive, carefully tended park, with copies of famous statues in white marble as well as a stained-glass version of Leonardo da Vinci's *Last Supper*, all surmounted by a greyish-white castle. You can acquire a stake in this curious park by purchasing share certificates financed by an instalment plan. In return, you have reserved for you a stylish burial place, and will be able to enjoy numerous copies of works of art and the 'largest Christian painting in America, depicting a thousand people'. Even Michelangelo's *David* stands in all his naked glory on the top of the hill — guaranteed not to fall down if an earthquake strikes! (His predecessor was felled by the earthquake of 1971 and broke several limbs.) Of course there are also the usual gift shops. Forest Lawn is a fascinating example of American culture, a striking mixture of fantastical death cult, kitsch, real estate deal, religious schmaltz and ostentatious pomp, in all of which the word 'death' is never mentioned, but is replaced by all manner of euphemisms and circumlocutions.

J. Paul Getty Museum (in Malibu, 17985 Pacific Coast Highway, Tues.–Sun., 10 am–5 pm). The unimaginably rich oil magnate lived here like an emperor, in a Roman-style mansion complete with fountains, screened by trees and filled with precious works of art, particularly Greek and Roman antiquities and European Baroque. Entry is free, but a parking place should be reserved in advance, by telephoning at least a week ahead (213 459 8402).

Griffith Park (at the foot of Mount Hollywood; Los Feliz Blvd and Riverside Drive, right next to Forest Lawn) is an oasis of green in an urban desert. You can play golf, examine the universe in the elegant observatory, attend open-air plays and concerts in the *Greek Theater* (2700 North Vermont Ave), wander through the highly regarded zoo and marvel at the technical wonders in the *Hall of Science*.

Hollywood. Hollywood! It looks like the rest of LA — dead straight roads and thundering freeways, gas stations, supermarkets, factories, characterless

The J. Paul Getty Museum

snow-white buildings, spindly palm trees, billboards and, now and again, a cinema. The old dream factory long ago expanded well beyond the boundaries of Hollywood, to Burbank, Culver City and Universal City, but the name has never lost its lure. Visitors of course see little of the city of film, since the studios are closed to the public (exceptions: Universal Studios and NBC Television Studios, 3000 West Alameda Ave – see pages 81 and 82). The chances of running into Faye Dunaway, Jane Fonda or Paul Newman in Hollywood are minimal. Contact with the stars is possible, however – at *Mann's Chinese Theater* (6925 Hollywood Blvd), where their hands and feet are imprinted in cement, and at the Hollywood *Wax Museum*, where you can see life-size replicas of your favourite stars (6767 Hollywood Blvd). And on *Hollywood Boulevard* there are star-shaped brasses bearing their names.

In summer the LA Philharmonic plays in the shell of the *Hollywood Bowl*,

an amphitheatre with 17,250 seats (tel. 213 876 8742).

Knott's Berry Farm (in Buena Park, 8039 Beach Blvd) is a fairground with three theme parks, based on a gold-diggers' town, the Roaring Twenties and a Mexican village at fiesta time. The name is a reminder of the park's origins in an old strawberry farm. The *Movieland Wax Museum and Palace of Living Art* (7711 Beach Blvd) has life-size displays of stars in famous film scenes.

La Brea Tar Pits and George C. Page Museum (Wilshire Blvd and Curson Ave) are probably the most astonishing attractions in LA, because they are utterly unique. How ironic it is that, in a city that prides itself on being a showcase for a wealthy, unrestrained, electronic, overwhelmingly technological future, the most exhilarating sight is a series of tar pits that turn out to be enormous prehistoric treasure-troves.

The museum, housed in a note-

Mann's Chinese Theater

worthy building, shows what has been trapped in the tar of Los Angeles since the ice age, only to be ejected again by the stinking, bubbling slime: elephants and lions, condors and eagles, bears, pumas and coyotes, whole herds of antelopes and camels, wolves, giant sloths and bisons. And large numbers of a terrifying, long-extinct beast, the sabre-toothed tiger. The oldest skeletons in the *Rancho La Brea* are about 40,000 years old, and all of them suffered the same grisly death by drowning in the blackish-brown, bubbling swamp. Inquisitive camels and antelopes probably tried to drink the brackish water – and became inescapably trapped in the tar. And then pumas, lions and tigers, eager to attack this defenceless prey, fell upon the panic-stricken animals, only to sink helplessly in their turn in the deadly morass. The museum shows how the asphalt swamp kept its victims for tens of thousands of years – millions of animals and plants and even a woman, buried since the ice age. As you stand in front of the massive skeleton of the Californian mammoth or watch scientists through plate-glass windows as they solve the mysteries of these prehistoric bones, this ancient death chamber will take your breath away. (Guided tours Tues.–Sun., 1 pm; the museum is in *Hancock Park*. Film presentations, observation platform.) The neighbouring *Los Angeles County Museum of Art* (5905 Wilshire Blvd) is recommended for art-lovers.

Marineland (in Palos Verdes, the stubby peninsula in the south of the municipality of LA) is an aquatic playground. Here you can dive with 2,000 different sea animals in an aquarium, feed the famous dolphins, watch a killer whale, laugh at circus tricks, have a picnic and even observe wild sea-lions.

Meet 'Jaws' in Hollywood

NBC Tour (in Burbank, 3000 West Alameda Ave, tel. 213 840 3572) is one of the opportunities to slip briefly under the almost impenetrable surface of the 'entertainment capital of the world'. Although the tour is aimed particularly at the American television audience, it is also of interest to European visitors, since NBC (National Broadcasting Corporation) is one of the three giants of American radio and television (the others are ABC and CBS). It begins every half-hour, lasts an hour and includes the sets of well-known television shows. If you want to be present at the recording of an NBC show, call 213 840 3537 for free tickets.

The Queen Mary, *Long Beach*

Olvera Street is the well-kept show-piece displaying LA's Mexican past. It is a pedestrian zone with arts and crafts shops, restored houses, fast-food restaurants where you can eat enchiladas, and a brick-paved imitation of a Mexican market (North Main St and *State Historic Park* with Visitors Center, 130 Paseo de la Plaza, tel. 628 1274).

Queen Mary (in Long Beach, a city of 365,000 inhabitants within Greater Los Angeles; an important port and much frequented for its six miles of beach, parts of which are less than well maintained). The pensioned-off British luxury liner has found its last mooring place here, where it is used as a hotel, conference centre and tourist attraction. A rather sad self-guided tour takes you through the machine rooms, upper deck and bridge of the liner, which was built in 1936; at 81,000 tons, it was one of the largest ships of its day. On display in a glass dome nearby is the *Spruce Goose*, the largest wooden aeroplane ever constructed (it was built for the millionaire Howard Hughes).

Six Flags Magic Mountain (in Valencia, half an hour by car north of

Hollywood, via Interstate 5 and 405) is a theme park which would hardly be worth the drive were it not for two sensational rides. The most exciting is 'Colossus', the largest, fastest and most hair-raising roller-coaster in the world, a snow-white monster, with fourteen apparently vertical precipices down which the cars rush at more than 60 mph (100 kph). The other one is 'The Revolution', an upright circle of steel rails, almost 100 ft (30 m) high. The cars thunder round a complete loop — nobody falls out, thanks to centrifugal force. The admission fee includes entry to all rides.

Universal Studios Tour (in Universal City, via Hollywood Freeway as far as Lankershim Blvd). A strictly organised operation which each day shepherds more than 10,000 visitors through Universal's studio lot. You stand in long queues, pay your admission fee, ride in trams, walk through a copy of Robert Wagner's wardrobe, sit in a (disused) film studio, marvel at sophisticated lighting and projection effects and drive through film sets. The 2½-hour tour is followed by the staging of various shows. Started by Universal in the

1960s, when the Hollywood studios were facing hard times, the tour has long since become a separate and very profitable activity in its own right. (For further information, phone 818 877 2121.)

Ex Excursions to the islands

Two hours by boat or fifteen minutes by air from Long Beach or LA Harbor is

Santa Catalina Island, a rocky but attractive island, a good 25 miles (40 km) long, which is a very popular and thus often overcrowded holiday destination, with beaches, marinas, tennis courts, golf courses, riding, flying fish, glass-bottomed boats and hire cars (you are not allowed to bring your own). The main town, *Avalon*, has a museum, pretty restaurants and airy fish-and-chip stands, facilities for diving and spearfishing, boat hire, boutiques and a casino. (Enquiries about boat and aeroplane connections from the LA region and about hotels – reservations strongly recommended – should be addressed to the *Avalon Chamber of Commerce*, 213 510 1520.)

Channel Island National Monument comprises three of the eight so-called Channel Islands, which lie west of LA and south of Santa Barbara. The three are *San Miguel, Anacapa* and *Santa Barbara Island*. Getting there is somewhat difficult, but the journey is very worth while for nature-lovers. On *Santa Barbara* there are large colonies of sea-lions, while on *Anacapa* thousands of pelicans and cormorants nest. There is no public transport, and no hotels; the crossing is by private boat. Camping is allowed here and there, but only with a permit. (Permits and information about boat connections can be obtained from the Superintendent, 1699 Anchors Way Drive, Ventura, CA 93003, tel. 805 644 8157.)

Going south

South of Los Angeles, one beach merges into another to form a recreation area over 60 miles (100 km) long.

Newport Beach has seven islands and 8,000 yachts, and transport in town is by boat. The Snowbirds Regatta is held in July, but in good weather the yachts race practically every weekend. There are six miles of beaches. The *Newport Dunes Aquatic Park* is good for picnics, open-air sport and various fairground amusements. Some really eccentric 'character boats' gather in Newport Beach in August for their own festival.

The *Spruce Goose, Long Beach*

Laguna Beach

Laguna Beach (pop. 19,000) is

famous for its art colony, with studios, galleries, *tableaux vivants*, flowers, exhibitions, and original and extravagant villas. In summer the pictures, sculptures and pottery of the resident artists go on show at the *Festival of Arts and Pageant of the Masters* (information: tel. 494 1147). Nearby *Irvine* has a safari park, in which elephants, lions, leopards, giraffes and other African animals roam freely while visitors drive past in their cars – with the windows tightly shut (*Lion Country Safari*, 8800 Irvine Center Drive).

Mission San Juan Capistrano in

San Juan Capistrano (pop. 24,000) is one of the most beautiful monasteries from which the Spanish colonised present-day California, subdued the Indians and taught them how to farm and raise cattle in the European manner. One of the two monastery churches

Mission San Juan Capistrano

built by the Franciscans (dedicated in 1778) has survived and is still in use. The ornate high altar in the Spanish Late Baroque style was brought from overseas. The building has suffered earthquake damage but has been well restored. For 100 years, the mission was famed for its annual miracle: on October 23rd, the name day of the church's patron saint, all the swallows flew away. One day, however, one of the *padres* discovered that *all* the swallows in the area fly south on the same day...

San Clemente (pop. 35,000)

was famous in the 1970s, when President Nixon had his house here (the White House West), from which he often conducted affairs of state.

The town has a wide beach, pretty, Mexican-style houses and a long pier for fishermen. In the vicinity is *Camp Pendleton*, the largest training centre of the American Marine Corps. The neighbouring *San Onofro Nuclear Generating Station* promotes its product, nuclear-generated electricity, by means of an exhibition and an educational film.

Palomar Mountain (6,140 ft/1,871

m) requires a detour (to the Cleveland National Forest, between the Pacific and the southern part of the Mojave Desert). The road winds high up the mountain to the *Palomar Observatory*, which is situated at a height of 5,574 ft (1,700 m). It is one of the largest and most famous observatories in the world; it houses the Hale Telescope. This truly gigantic instrument which has a mirror diameter of 17 ft ¾ in (5.2 m) seems to float in a silver dome twelve storeys high. Its range – a billion light-years into the universe – is almost inconceivable. Of course you cannot take a look for yourself, but there is a visitors' gallery and an exhibition of photographs taken by the telescope.

America's dream road

The road leads from Los Angeles to San Francisco, from the palm trees of the south to the redwoods of the north, a journey of about twelve hours' driving time, offering fabulous views of the ocean and the mountains. It is the coast road, a combination of US 101 and Hwy 1, which leave LA as separate roads, meet in Oxnard and run together as far as Gaviota. They then diverge, come together again in Grover City and finally separate for the last time north of San Luis Obispo. From here, US 101 leads in a straight line to Salinas, while Hwy 1 becomes the actual 'dream road', following the coast from Morro Bay to Big Sur. This is America's westernmost road: no gas stations, no campsites, no inns, just panoramic views, down into the foaming sea breaking against steep cliffs, up into the ravines of the Santa Lucia Range.

Ventura (pop. 83,000)

was the ninth of the twenty-one missions established by the Spanish Franciscans. The San Buenaventura mission (1782) has been well restored. Beach, marina, surfing. Boat trips to the Channel Islands.

Santa Barbara (pop. 79,000)

The Spanish influence has been retained and even enhanced in its Old Town. The town was once the 'Queen of the Missions' (Los Olivos and Laguna St; 1786). It is now a pleasant, carefully kept town, with numerous cultural and sporting activities, strict building regulations, no industry, a surprisingly good art gallery (*Museum of Art,* 1130 State St), an excellent beach, a yacht harbour and an unusually large number of different species of bird, which is why it has a reputation as a birdwatchers' paradise. It is an obviously prosperous town, a

place for retired people and holiday-makers, with an equable, mainly sunny

Santa Barbara Courthouse

climate, even in the winter months. The *County Courthouse* (1120 Anacapa St) is a lavish building in a strange but much-admired mixture of styles. A sightseeing walk is made easier by the *Red Tiles*, which lead walkers to the town's showpieces; several hours are required for a complete tour.

Between Santa Barbara and the *Santa Ynez* peninsula, one beach follows another: *Goleta, El Capitan, Gaviota*. Goleta is home to part of the University of California, art galleries and a botanical sight of tropical splendour, *Dos Pueblos Orchid Ranch*, about 8 miles (13 km) west, near the road.

At Gaviota, Hwy 1 leaves US 101 and winds through the Santa Ynez peninsula. Its course takes it close to *Vandenberg Air Force Base*, not only one of the largest and most important bases of the American Air Force, but also a major space centre. *Lompoc* is of interest because of its enchantingly colourful flower fields and the splendidly restored *Mission La Purisma* (1787–1813).

San Luis Obispo (pop. 38,000)

The cones of two volcanoes rise above the town, which like Santa Barbara and

Ventura owes its existence to a Franciscan mission, in this case San Luis Obispo de Tolosa (1772, Chorro and Monterey Sts). Places of interest include the shop of the Sinsheimer brothers, which dates from 1876 and is preserved in the style of that time, and the Madonna Inn. The town centre was severely damaged in the 1989 earthquake. In August there is a six-day Mozart Festival. *Avila Beach* and *Pismo Beach* are popular with surfers, anglers, sailors (hire-boats) and swimmers.

Hwy 1 finally goes it alone in Morro Bay, leaving US 101 to run in a straight line through fertile salad-, artichoke- and potato-growing country to King City and Salinas.

Morro Bay has a silhouette that is as unmistakable as that of New York. The second largest rock in the world, *Morro Rock*, towers 575 ft (175 m) out of the sea.

It is here that the actual coast road starts and the highly industrialised twentieth century is left behind. Soon there are no more side-roads, at the most sandy tracks which quickly end in scrub. At first there are a few resorts – *Cayucos*, which is a modest place, and *Cam-*

bria, somewhat prettier. The next thing you will see is a massive car-park, together with ticket booths, a large gift shop with an extraordinary range of junk, and buses which take visitors up to America's largest gingerbread palace: the Hearst-San Simeon State Historical Monument, better known as *Hearst Castle*, the hill-top fantasy castle built by the newspaper tycoon William Randolph Hearst, the multi-millionaire with a passion for everything artistic. The castle was begun in 1919 and Hearst died in 1951, with 'La Casa Grande' still uncompleted. It presents a dazzling clash of architectural styles: classical columns mingle with Spanish, Gothic and Moorish elements, the swimming pool is a Graeco-Roman pastiche, there is a guest-house in the Renaissance style and the library is Tuscan in inspiration. The antiques, however, are genuine: they cost Hearst $50 million. If you wish to visit the castle you must go on a guided tour. Tickets are often sold out weeks in advance in high season. There are several tours, each lasting about two hours.

The best section of *Scenic Highway One* is about 60 miles (100 km) long; it hugs the coastline, flanked on one side by the Santa Lucia Mountain Range, rising to more than 6,500 ft (2,000 m), and on the other by the rocky Pacific coast. Its vertiginous bridges and hair-raising bends make it a popular location for Hollywood film-makers shooting breakneck car chases. In real life, it is a nature conservancy area with fabulous views.

A special tip

Big Sur is a happy hunting ground for apostles of all kinds, for artists and flower-children, for millionaires and hikers, poets, drop-outs, ecologists, philosophers, architects and masters of the art of living. Their dwellings are discreet and are usually concealed in the apparently untouched landscape. At *Pfeiffer Big Sur State Park* you can rent simple wooden huts; there are hiking trails, places to build campfires, beaches, unspoiled countryside, and good restaurants such as *Ventana* and *Nepenthe*.

Lone Cypress, Monterey Bay

Shopping in Carmel

Carmel (pop. 5,000)

appears elegant and expensive, with smart shops and restaurants – a prosperous village in lush countryside, right next to the sea, like a secret address. Nothing of the kind: Carmel is just about California's favourite place. It also has a past, as the Mission San Carlos Borromeo del Rio Carmelo. Father Junipero Serra, founder of the Californian missions, lived out the last years of his life here; he died in 1784. He is buried in the church, near the pulpit. Carmel hit the headlines a few years ago because of the election of Hollywood star Clint Eastwood to the office of mayor.

Monterey (pop. 31,000)

Several golf courses, a harbour pier with shops and bars, a pretty little Old Town, a beautiful bay, even a place in world literature: Monterey has been pampered since the time it was capital of Spanish, then Mexican and later American California. John Steinbeck immortalised *Cannery Row*, a real road lined with canning factories. The buildings are still standing, but without the fish. For something strange happened, a catastrophe for Monterey, a mystery for marine biologists and lay people alike: the shoals of sardines which were the livelihood of Cannery Row and Monterey suddenly disappeared, never to return. The warehouses of Cannery Row now house restaurants, boutiques, art galleries and antique-shops. If you follow the yellow and red *Path of History* signs painted on the street, you will pass all the historic buildings in about an hour's walk. At the west end of Cannery Row is the *Monterey Bay Aquarium*, the largest exhibit aquarium in the USA. The building is on the site of an old sardine cannery, and the displays include a three-storey kelp forest housed in an acrylic tank holding over 300,000 gallons of seawater. The aquarium is also a sanctuary for orphaned sea otters rescued from the wild.

If you pay the toll you can drive around the *Monterey Peninsula* along the private road of *Seventeen Mile Drive*, famous for its magnificent landscapes and seascapes. You pass first through a luxurious residential estate, then you will see the sea, a golf course, cypresses and sand, and then you will come to *Seal Rock*, a rocky island crowded with seals and sea-birds, a scene unrivalled by any zoo. Monterey is a busy place: in January there is the Bing Crosby Golf Tournament, in July Clint Eastwood's Celebrity Tennis Tournament, in September the Monterey Jazz Festival and in December the California Wine Festival. In autumn, it is aflutter with the brightly coloured wings of the millions of orange butterflies that migrate to escape from the cold northern winter.

Santa Cruz (pop. 47,000)

has become famous for its active environmental protection policies. Residents helped to restore the run-down Pacific Garden Mall, making it one of the gems of the town – until the 1989 earthquake struck, necessitating further rebuilding. The beach has natural bridges – arches of sandstone eroded by the sea.

The Central Valley

The Central Valley is a gigantic basin more than 435 miles (700 km) long and more than 40 miles (65 km) wide; it is also known as *Big Valley*. The valley is sealed top and bottom like a sausage: to the north, near *Redding*, the *Coast Range* and *Sierra Nevada* touch, while to the south the *Tehachapi Mountains* rise up to close the valley off from the *Mojave Desert*.

The valley is hot. Where there is no natural irrigation nature has been given a helping hand, with astonishing success. The Central Valley, California's Garden of Eden, is rightly considered one of the richest agricultural areas in the world. There is no fruit or vegetable that does not grow here: lettuces, dates, strawberries, artichokes, grapes, asparagus, oranges, lemons, olives, melons, broccoli, corn, almonds, plums, hops, peaches, apricots, spinach, pears. To say nothing of tobacco and cotton.

You can drive quickly through the valley. The roads are wide and dead straight. Orchards and vegetable fields flash past. Acres of flowers slide by in a colourful blur. For hours on end, California's rich abundance whirls past the window of your hurrying car. There is not much point getting out. It's very hot. Fresno? Not a lot to see there. Bakersfield? Merced? Modesto? A region of extraordinary fertility – but monotonous. For tourists, the 'Big Valley' is a transit region with an excellent road network.

Bakersfield (pop. 153,000)

is the centre of the southern part of the Central Valley (*San Joaquin Valley*). The agricultural abundance of the area has determined the growth of the town and its amenities. The *Kern County Museum* (3801 Chester Ave) incorporates *Pioneer Village*, which includes genuine buildings from the Wild West period. The *Kern River Canyon* is worth looking at as you drive past.

Fresno (pop. 294,000)

The fertility of the surrounding Fresno County breaks many records. It is America's premier agricultural area, containing the largest artificially irrigated area of farmland in the USA, as well as the largest winery (Cibrari). Vineyards, cotton-fields and fig-growing form the basis of the city's prosperity.

Merced (pop. 49,000)

is the most convenient entry point for *Yosemite National Park*. There is a bus shuttle service between the park and the station, airport and bus station.

Modesto (pop. 185,000)

is the archetypal American provincial town, prosperous, respectable, proud of the remnants of its brief and somewhat uneventful past. There is a museum (*McHenry Museum*, 1402 I St) and also *Miller's California Ranch* with old cars, shops and tools.

Stockton (pop. 132,000)

is notable for its canal, which links it to San Francisco Bay. 930 miles (1,500 km) of navigable waterways are accessible from Stockton. Boats can be hired.

Angel's Camp (pop. 2,500)

is famous as the setting of Mark Twain's short story 'Jim Smiley's Famous Jumping Frog', written in 1865. And now, every May, a jumping-frog competition is held. There is also a museum, and white-water canoeing.

Useful things to know: for all visitors

Facts and figures

California (abbreviated to Calif. or Cal. and, with zip codes, to CA) is one of the *Pacific States* in the far west of the USA; the others are Washington and Oregon. It borders the Pacific Ocean in the west, Nevada and Arizona to the east and Mexico to the south. With over 28 million inhabitants in 1988, it is the most populous state in the Union; approximately one in every ten Americans lives in California. It is the third largest state (after Alaska and Texas), with an area of 158,706 sq miles (411,047 sq km). California stretches for about 800 miles (1,300 km) from 42° north (about the same latitude as Rome) to 32° 30″ (about the same latitude as Tripoli).

The state capital is Sacramento. The Governor is elected every four years, as are the Secretary of State, Treasurer (Finance Minister), Attorney-General and Superintendent of Public Instruction (Minister of Education). The state parliament has two chambers, the *Senate* (forty senators, elected to serve for four years) and the *Assembly* (eighty assemblymen, elected for two years). The state is divided into fifty-eight counties.

The school system is regarded as one of the best in the USA, with the University of California at the top of the pyramid (it has campuses at Berkeley, San Diego, Los Angeles, San Francisco and Santa Barbara, among other places). Two private universities, Stanford in Palo Alto and the University of Southern California in Los Angeles, are also world renowned.

The state's prosperity is based largely on agriculture, which flourishes particularly in the extremely fertile *Central Valley*, 74% of which is artificially irrigated.

The most important products are wheat, sugar-beet, cotton, grapes and wine, fruit (particularly citrus fruit), and vegetables of all kinds. Forests cover 41% of the state, and California is one of the major timber-producing areas of the USA. Other flourishing industries include fishing, livestock production, oil and gas, and tourism. Since the Second World War, the aerospace industry has come to the fore and now employs one-third of all industrial workers in the state. Other important industrial sectors include mechanical and electrotechnical engineering, metals and chemicals, film and television, and electronics.

California has more than 150,000 miles (250,000 km) of roads and 235 airports. The largest ports are San Francisco, Oakland, San Diego (naval base), Los Angeles and Long Beach.

The largest minority ethnic group is made up of immigrants from Mexico; 8% of the population is black and 0.3% Asian and native American.

The Californian state colours are blue and gold, while the state symbols are the golden poppy and the sequoia. The state motto is 'Eureka' ('I've found it!'). The state anthem begins with the words 'I love you, California'.

Climate

The state is divided into two quite distinct climatic zones, the cool, rainy north (average July temperature in Eureka 56°F/13.5°C, annual precipitation 38.5 in/980 mm) and the hot, dry south (average June temperature in San Diego 70.5°F/21.4°C, annual precipitation 10.4 in/264 mm). North of San Francisco the temperature of the sea never rises above 63°F/17°C, while south of Los Angeles it can reach 72.5°F/22.5°C in summer.

Travelling to California

The major European airlines fly direct to Los Angeles and San Francisco. Both cities, and San Diego, are linked by a dense network of direct flights to virtually all the major cities in America.

The railways once made California great, but today they play only a subsidiary role in the transport system. *Amtrak*, the national passenger rail carrier, has three famous trains that link California to more eastern parts of the country. The *San Francisco Zephyr* comes from Chicago, the *Southwest Limited* travels between Los Angeles and Chicago using the southern route through Arizona and New Mexico, and the *Sunset Limited* links Los Angeles with New Orleans. The trains have modern double-decker coaches with observation decks. The journeys last several days; tickets must be booked in advance and seats reserved.

If you are travelling by rail to California – and the western USA in general – it is worth buying a USARAIL card, which must be purchased before you leave home.

Discount passes are also sold by the two big bus companies: *Greyhound* has the *Ameripass*, while its competitor, *Continental Trailways*, has the *Eagle Pass*. This is the cheapest way of travelling, if you have the time. (Your travel agent can make the bookings.)

Medical care and insurance

Medical care in California is very good. It is also very expensive. Since treatment and medication costs must be paid immediately, it is essential to have adequate insurance cover. (Information from your travel agent.)

Clothes

For Los Angeles and southern California, light summer clothes are in order. For the desert regions, dress as lightly as possible. San Francisco and the north can often be cool even in summer, and light woollen jumpers and a raincoat are recommended. Smart restaurants, particularly in San Francisco, usually insist on men wearing a jacket and tie.

Reservations

Hotel reservations are valid until 6 pm, unless you have specifically arranged a later arrival time. However, there are also *guaranteed reservations*. To make these you quote your credit card number; then if you do not turn up the hotel will charge the cost of the room to your account.

Car rental

The cheapest way to hire a car is to book it through one of the large car-hire companies before you leave home. If you are planning to drive long distances, make sure your contract includes unlimited mileage. As well as the large, internationally known car-hire companies, there are many smaller firms, which often undercut their larger rivals. Within the USA, you can call most of the car rental companies free of charge in order to make enquiries and reservations:

Avis   800 331 1212
Budget   800 527 0700
Dollar   800 421 6868
Value   800 327 2501
Hertz   800 654 3131
National   800 328 4567
Thrifty   800 367 2277
American International   800 527 0202

There are reduced rates at weekends, and sometimes special offers. Fuel is paid for by the user. Not included in the rental price are personal accident insurance and collision damage waiver. You should check with the company whether the car can be taken out of the state, and whether it can be returned to a different branch of the company.

Safety precautions

California is by no means as dangerous as is often maintained. Nevertheless, caution is required. The police strongly urge tourists to avoid empty streets, parks and port areas at night. Do not buy any watches, cameras or jewels on the streets. Do not give your hotel address to people you do not know. Carry only small amounts of cash on you. Bolt your door at night and use the security chain; do not answer a knock if you are not expecting a visit.

Useful things to know: for overseas visitors

Immigration and customs

The American Immigration Service requires all travellers entering the USA to be in possession of a valid passport. British passport-holders do not need a

The Ponderosa Ranch, Incline Village

visa, but many other visitors do; ask at a US consulate or embassy. The visa is valid indefinitely, but the stay in the USA must not last longer than three months. The passport must be valid for a further six months after that. Persons with a visitor's visa may not enter paid employment in the USA.

American customs can be awkward. Count on having to open at least one suitcase and display its contents. Plants and plant cuttings, meat products and fruit may not be imported. You may bring in presents up to a value of $100, as well as 200 cigarettes or 50 cigars, and 1 litre of spirits.

Time differences

California is eight hours behind Greenwich Mean Time. Together with the neighbouring states of Washington, Oregon and Nevada, it is on *Pacific Standard Time*, one of the four time zones in the USA. The time difference between California and New York, Washington DC and Boston is three hours. (At 5 pm GMT it is 12 noon in New York and 9 am in San Francisco.) Summer time, or *daylight saving time*, is in force in the USA between the first Sunday in April and the last Sunday in October. Since these dates do not coincide exactly with British Summer Time, there are days when the time differences are an hour less.

Currency

The unit of currency is of course the *US dollar* ($). One dollar = 100 cents. It is often difficult to change foreign currency in the USA, since not many banks are used to such transactions, but traveller's cheques issued by the major international (particularly American) financial institutions are accepted everywhere. A credit card (American Express, Visa, MasterCard) is very useful.

The dollar is simple to use, but there

Big Sur Highway

is one catch: all banknotes are the same shape and colour, making it easy to mistake a $5 bill for a $100 one. The following notes are in circulation: $1, $5, $10, $20, $50 and $100 bills.

Coins, on the other hand, differ in size, appearance and colour. Penny: 1 cent; nickel: 5 cents; dime: 10 cents; quarter: 25 cents; half dollar: 50 cents. There is a $1 coin, but it is seldom seen.

Weights and measures

The American system of weights and measures is essentially the same as that used in Britain. There are, however, some differences. The US gallon, for example, is equivalent to only 0.83 of a British gallon (or 3.79 litres).

The technological age is exerting some influence and America is slowly adapting to the metric system, although there is a long way to go yet. In California, many distances are indicated in kilometres as well as miles.

Public holidays

Many places are closed on public holidays, so take these into account when planning your travels. Over long weekends, such as those associated with Memorial Day and Labor Day, accommodation is usually in short supply. The holidays are as follows:

New Year's Day (January 1st); *Washington's Birthday* (third Monday in February); *Memorial Day* (last Monday in May); *Independence Day* (July 4th, the principal national holiday, with fireworks and overcrowding in all holiday resorts!); *Labor Day* (first Monday in September); *Columbus Day* (second Monday in October); *Thanksgiving* (fourth Thursday in November); *Christmas Day* (December 25th). Good Friday, Easter Monday, Whit Monday and Boxing Day are *not* public holidays in the USA.

Post and telephone

Stamps can be bought at post offices, and also from stamp machines in large hotels. You cannot telephone or telegraph from post offices; to send a telegram, go to a Western Union office. To telephone the UK from a payphone or private phone, dial 011 44 and omit initial 0 from area code.

Tipping

In bars the bill comes without the service charge, so you should leave 15% of the bill as a tip, subject to a minimum of 25 cents ($1 in more up-market establishments). In smart restaurants and nightclubs, the rule is to leave 20% of the bill as a tip, or alter the credit card slip with a ballpoint pen to include the extra.

You should give hotel porters at least 50 cents per item of luggage they carry up to your room. Taxi-drivers expect 15%, ladies' hairdressers $2 (at least) and the hat-check girl 50 cents per person. Hotel doormen also expect 50 cents when they call you a taxi. Chambermaids receive 50 cents per night, and the cigarette vendor in nightclubs also gets 50 cents. It is not the practice to tip at gas stations, and the desk clerk in hotels will not expect anything either.

Taxis

Hardly anybody says *taxi* – they are almost always called *cabs*. Since cars and petrol ('gas') cost less in the USA, taxi fares are somewhat lower than in the UK. At most airports posters now inform travellers of the cost of a ride into town, to prevent overcharging. Away from the airports there are hardly any taxi ranks – you simply hail a cab from the side of the road. If you are alone or with just one companion, the long journey from the airport to the city centre is significantly cheaper by bus (except in San Diego, where the airport is close to the city centre).

Electricity

The standard electricity supply in the USA is 110 volts, compared with 240 volts in the UK. Consequently, electrical appliances designed for use in the UK and not fitted with dual-voltage capability will require a voltage transformer. These can be purchased before leaving home, although converter kits can also be bought in the USA. American wall sockets do not take British plugs; adaptors can be bought before leaving home, but can also be obtained in drugstores in America.

Important addresses
Diplomatic offices

British Embassy
3100 Massachusetts Ave NW
Washington DC 20008;
tel. 202 462 1340

British Consulate
1 Sansome Street
San Francisco; tel. 415 981 3030

3701 Wilshire Blvd
Los Angeles; tel. 213 385 7381

Canadian Embassy
1746 Massachusetts Ave NW
Washington DC 20036;
tel. 202 785 1400

Australian Embassy
1601 Massachusetts Ave NW
Washington DC 20036;
tel. 202 797 3000

New Zealand Embassy
37 Observatory Cir. NW
Washington DC 20008;
tel. 202 328 4800

Irish Embassy
2234 Massachusetts Ave NW
Washington DC 20008;
tel. 202 462 3939

Tourist information
In US

United States Travel and Tourism Administration (USTTA)
Department of Commerce
14th Street NW
Washington DC 20230;
tel. 202 377 0136

California Office of Tourism
1121 L Street, Suite 103
Sacramento, CA 95814;
tel. 916 322 1396

In UK

USTTA
Travel Information Centre
22 Sackville Street
London W1X 2EA; tel. 071 439 7433

Index

Anacapa   83
Angel's Camp   89
Avila Beach   86

Badwater   64
Bakersfield   19, **89**
Barstow   66
Berkeley   42f., 90
Big Sur   87
Bolinas   42
Brawley   67

Calexico   67
Calico Ghost Town   66
Calistoga   45, 46
Carmel   88
Central Valley   6, 16, 19 46, **89**, 90
Channel Island National Monument   83
Channel Islands   13

Dante's View   64
Death Valley   63ff.
Devil's Cornfield   63
Devil's Golf Course   64

El Capitan   12, **58**
El Centro   67
Empire Mine State Historic Park   54
Eureka   50

Fort Bragg   48
Fort Ross   10
Fresno   89
Furnace Creek   64

Golden Canyon   64
Goleta   86
Grant Grove   60, 61
Grass Valley   54

Hearst Castle   87
Humboldt Redwood State Park   48f.

Imperial Valley   67
Incline Village   56

Joshua Tree National Monument   67

Keeler   61
Kings Canyon National Park   13, **60f.**
Klamath National Forest   50

Laguna Beach   20, **84**
Lake Shasta Caverns   51
Lake Tahoe   11, 55
Las Vegas   69
Lassen Volcanic National Park   51f.
Lava Beds National Monument   51
Lee Vining   57
Leo Carillo State Beach   20
Lompoc   86
Lone Pine   61
Los Angeles   6, 11, 13, 17, 20, **74ff.**, 90
  Arboretum   78
  Chinatown   78
  City Hall   75, 78
  Civic Center   75, **78**
  Disneyland   78f.
  Farmers Market   79
  Forest Lawn Memorial Park   79
  J. Paul Getty Museum   79
  Greek Theater   79
  Griffith Park   79
  Hall of Science   79
  Hollywood   4, 5, **79f.**
  Knott's Berry Farm   80
  La Brea Tar Pits and George C. Page Museum   80f.
  Long Beach   5, 90
  Marineland   81
  Music Center   75, 78
  NBC (National Broadcasting Corporation)   81
  Olvera Street   82

  Queen Mary   82
  Six Flags Magic Mountain   4, **82**
  Universal Studios   82f.
Los Padres National Forest   13

Mendocino   48
Merced   89
Mexicali   67
Modesto   89
Mojave Desert   66f.
Mono Lake   57
Monterey   10, **88**
Morro Bay   86
Mount Shasta   51
Mount Whitney   61
Muir Woods National Monument   15, 41

Napa Valley   19, **45f.**
Nevada City   55
Newport Beach   83f.

Oakland   **43f.**, 90

Pacific Crest Trail   12
Palm Springs   68
Palo Alto   **44**, 90
Palomar Mountain   84
Pismo Beach   86
Point Reyes   48
Point Reyes Beach   42
Ponderosa Ranch   56

Randsburg   67
Redding   51
Redwood National Park   50
Reno (Nevada)   56

Sacramento   6, **52f.**, 90
Saint Helena   45
Salton Sea   67
San Bernardino   68
San Clemente   84
San Diego   4, 5, 6, 11, 20, **70ff.**, 90

San Francisco   4, 5, 6, 8, 10, 11, 13, 15, 17, 20, **23ff.**, 90
Alcatraz   27, **28**
Bay Bridge   27, **28**
Cannery   30f.
Chinatown   23, **28f.**
City Hall   30
Civic Center   26, **30**
Coit Tower   35f.
Embarcadero Center   30
Fairmont   33f.
Ferry Building   26, **30**
Financial District   23
Fisherman's Wharf   26, **30**
Fort Point   35
Ghirardelli Square   31
Golden Gate   23
Golden Gate Bridge   23, 26, 27, **32**, 41
Golden Gate Park   27, **32f.**
Japantown   39
Mission Dolores   33
Museums   38
Nob Hill   26, **33**
North Beach   35
Palace of Fine Arts   35

Presidio   34f.
Russian Hill   10
Seal Rock   26
Telegraph Hill   35f.
Transamerica Pyramid   30, **37**
Twin Peaks   37
Union Square   37f.
San Joaquin Valley   19
San José (de Guadalupe)   6, **44**
San Juan Capistrano   6, **84**
San Luis Obispo   86
San Miguel   83
San Rafael   42
Santa Barbara   6, 19, **85f.**, 90
Santa Barbara Island   83
Santa Catalina Island   83
Santa Clara   6
Santa Cruz   6, **88**
Santa Monica   6, 20
Sausalito   27, **41**
Scotty's Castle   65
Sequoia National Park   12, 13, **60f.**
Shasta Dam   51
Shasta Lake   51
Shasta State Historic Park   51

Sierra National Forest   60
Sierra Nevada   5, 6, 11, 13, **54ff.**
Silver Lake   13
Sonoma   19, 46
South Lake Tahoe   55
Squaw Valley   12, 56
Stateline   55
Stinson Beach   42
Stockton   89
Sutter's Fort   7, 53

Tahoe City   56
Tahoe National Forest   56
Tijuana   13, **73**
Tomales Bay   48
Tropico Gold Mine   67

Ubehebe Crater   65

Vandenberg   5, 86
Ventura   20, 85

Yosemite National Park   4, 12, 13, **57ff.**

Zabriskie Point   64
Zephyr Cove   56

Original German text: Friedrich Müller. Translation: Andrew Wilson in association with First Edition Translations Ltd, Cambridge
Series editor, English edition: Jane Rolph

© Verlag Robert Pfützner GmbH, München. Original German edition

© Jarrold Publishing, Norwich, Great Britain 1/91. English language edition worldwide

Published in the US and Canada by Hunter Publishing, Inc.,
300 Raritan Center Parkway, Edison NJ 08818

Illustrations: G. Banks page 87; J. Allan Cash Ltd pages 11, 36, 41; James Davis Photography pages 31, 52 (top); Douglas Dickins page 33; Ema-Samm International pages 7 (both), 18, 35, 54, 57, 84; Eye Catchers page 16; A. Hawkins pages 8, 21, 70, 72, 73; R. Lake pages 82, 83; R. Johnson pages 5, 20, 34, 38, 53 (top), 58, 77, 80; S. Johnson pages 22, 32, 53 (bottom), 86, 88, 93; Audience Planners pages 50, 52 (bottom), 69; I. Thorpe pages 51, 59, 64; World Pictures (Feature-Pix) pages 1, 3, 19, 23, 42, 45, 47, 60, 63, 65, 68, 79.

The publishers have made every endeavour to ensure the accuracy of this publication but can accept no responsibility for any errors or omissions. They would, however, appreciate notification of any inaccuracies to correct future editions.

Printed in Italy

ISBN 0–7117–0481–3